MODERN WITCHCRAFT AND MAGIC FOR BEGINNERS

A Guide to Traditional and Contemporary Paths, with Magical Techniques for the Beginner Witch

LISA CHAMBERLAIN

Modern Witchcraft and Magic for Beginners

Published by **Chamberlain Publications**

ISBN-13: 978-1-542614-40-5

Disclaimer

YOUR FREE GIFT

Thank you for adding this book to your Wiccan library! To learn more, why not join Lisa's Wiccan community and get an exclusive, free spell book?

The book is a great starting point for anyone looking to try their hand at practicing magic. The ten beginner-friendly spells can help you to create a positive atmosphere within your home, protect yourself from negativity, and attract love, health, and prosperity.

Little Book of Spells is now available to read on your laptop, phone, tablet, Kindle or Nook device!

To download, simply visit the following link:

www.wiccaliving.com/bonus

GET THREE
FREE AUDIOBOOKS
FROM LISA CHAMBERLAIN

Did you know that all of Lisa's books are available in audiobook format? Best of all, you can get **three audiobooks completely free** as part of a 30-day trial with Audible.

Wicca Starter Kit contains three of Lisa's most popular books for beginning Wiccans, all in one convenient place. It's the best and easiest way to learn more about Wicca while also taking audiobooks for a spin! Simply visit:

www.wiccaliving.com/free-wiccan-audiobooks

Alternatively, *Spellbook Starter Kit* is the ideal option for building your magical repertoire using candle and color magic, crystals and mineral stones, and magical herbs. Three spellbooks —over 150 spells—are available in one free volume, here:

www.wiccaliving.com/free-spell-audiobooks

Audible members receive free audiobooks every month, as well as exclusive discounts. It's a great way to experiment and see if audiobook learning works for you.

If you're not satisfied, you can cancel anytime within the trial period. You won't be charged, and you can still keep your books!

CONTENTS

Introduction 11

Part One: Ancient Wisdom in Modern Times 13

  Witchcraft Today 14

  What Witchcraft *Is* (and Isn't) 15

    All Around the World.. 15

    Closer to Home.. 17

  A Brief History of Western "Witchcraft" 19

    In the Beginning 20

    The Invention of "Witches".. 22

    Enlightenment and Revival.. 24

  So Is Witchcraft Really an Ancient Religion?...................... 27

    A Few Modern Misconceptions...................................... 33

  A Diversity of Paths... 36

Part Two: Forms of Contemporary Witchcraft........................37

  Branches of the Craft... 38

  Paganism: The Umbrella's Umbrella 39

  The Many Definitions of "Traditional Witchcraft" 41

  1. Traditional Witchcraft 43

    Folk Healers.. 44

    Hereditary Witches 47

    Reconstructionists 48

  2. Traditionalist Witchcraft 50

The Feri Tradition 52

Cochrane's Craft 53

1734 54

Stregheria 55

Sabbatic Craft 56

Modern "Traditions" 57

Distinguishing "Wicca" from "Traditional" and
"Wiccan" from "Witch" 58

Wicca and Deity 59

Wicca and Reincarnation 62

Wicca and Correspondences 63

Wicca and "The Wheel of the Year" 64

Wicca And Ritual 65

Other Specifically Wiccan Practices 68

The Wiccan Moral Code 71

Respecting the Differences 73

Contemporary Witchcraft: Witchdom for the
21ˢᵗ Century 74

What is an Eclectic Witch? 74

Other Avenues of Contemporary Witchcraft 77

Hedgewitchery 78

Green Witchery 79

Kitchen Witchery 80

Natural Complements 82

The Many Ways of the Witch 83

**Part Three: Spirituality and Magic in
Contemporary Witchcraft** 85

Observance and Practice 86

Common Beliefs in Traditional Witchcraft Systems 90

Animism 90

Nature as Sacred Space 92

Non-Physical Entities 94

Spirits.. 94

Deities 98

The Otherworld... 100

Non-Deist Pantheism.. 101

Atheist Witchcraft: Hermeticism and Quantum Physics..... 102

The Hermetic Principles 103

The Principle of Mentalism... 104

The Principle of Correspondence 105

The Principle of Vibration... 106

Other Components of the Hermetic System................. 108

Science Catches Up with the "Old Religion" 109

The Unified Field... 110

Concepts and Uses of Magic in the Modern World.......... 112

Nature as Co-Creator 113

Aims of Magic.. 117

Witchcraft and Ethics 118

Witches Were Never Saints... 119

Black and White Magic.. 121

The Energy of Intention... 122

A Closer Look 124

Part Four: Exploring Your Inner Witch 125

Getting Started... 126

Creative Visualization 128

Visualization for Attuning to Magical Energy................. 128

Invocation 132

Invocation for Finding a Spirit Helper........................... 132

Candle Magic 135

Candle Spell for Inner Peace 136

Continuing on Your Journey..138

Conclusion 139

Suggestions for Further Reading...................................141
Three Free Audiobooks Promotion 142
More Books by Lisa Chamberlain...............................143
Free Gift Reminder 145

INTRODUCTION

"Witchcraft" is a word that, for some, may inspire fantastical images of women flying through the night sky on broomsticks and shooting sparks out of a glimmering wand, or dark-robed, mysterious figures dropping snakes and toads into bubbling cauldrons.

Other people take the word more seriously, but in an unfortunate way—mistakenly assuming that those who practice Witchcraft are actively seeking to cause illnesses, accidents, and other forms of trouble to anyone they dislike.

Of course, none of these notions are accurate—they are rooted in old fairy tales, Hollywood movies, and stubborn, persistent misconceptions that still cloud many people's understanding of this timeless and magical way of life.

If you're reading this, you most likely know that Witchcraft is not fantasy, and that it is not inherently malicious. Perhaps the images that come to mind for you when you hear the word "Witchcraft" are of candle light, crystals, and magical symbols, or charm satchels and colorful amulets, or fresh green herbs gathered under a Full Moon.

If so, then you're already on the right track to understanding the truth about Witchcraft—that it is a vibrant, nature-based spiritual practice that is alive and well in our modern times, just as it has been for longer than we've been recording history.

You're also probably aware that Witches generally tend not to be inclined to go around "hexing" people, but rather work to benefit their lives and the lives of those around them.

It's also fairly likely that you've had inklings, on and off throughout your life, that there's something just a little bit different about you—

something about the way you perceive the world that isn't quite shared by most people around you, but is difficult for you to explain. Maybe you sometimes get hunches, or premonitions, about things that shortly come to pass. Or, perhaps whenever you find yourself in a quiet, natural environment, such as a patch of woods, you sense another presence there—invisible and silent, but there nonetheless.

In fact, if you're reading this book, it's likely that you have more than once felt a sense that there's another layer of reality underneath what you can observe with your five senses, and that somehow you are meant to learn to understand it, if you can only find the right resources and the right path. If so, this guide is a great place to start your search.

Even if your curiosity is more intellectual than spiritual, you'll find plenty of useful information in these pages. The guide begins with an overview of the historical and cultural contexts from which contemporary Witchcraft has evolved, as well as the general beliefs and observances, rooted in the natural world, that characterize the widely varied forms and expressions of this dynamic spiritual practice.

You'll then be introduced to the core concepts, discovered in antiquity and used for centuries to explain the "why" and "how" of *magic*—another often misunderstood word for the phenomena that govern the workings of the Universe, and our abilities to direct energies with our personal power to achieve desired effects.

Finally, you'll get a brief introduction to the practice of "the Craft," as it's often called, through a look at a few common forms of magic as well as some example workings for you to try your hand at, if you feel so inclined. The end of the guide offers some suggested references for further reading, should you decide to pursue your interest in Witchcraft even further.

Congratulations on embarking on this delightful and enlightening journey!

Blessed Be.

PART ONE

ANCIENT WISDOM IN MODERN TIMES

WITCHCRAFT TODAY

Like many "New Age" or "occult" topics, Witchcraft is not easy to define, and, as hinted at in the Introduction to this guide, it's often quite misunderstood.

The fact that the Craft has roots dating back centuries doesn't seem to help much, since it was obviously misunderstood in those days as well—just look at the history of the persecution of Witches (and people merely *suspected* of being Witches) in Europe and North America over the past several hundred years!

Indeed, even today, though Western society is far more tolerant of differing religious and spiritual traditions, many who identify as Witches must still keep their beliefs and practices a secret from their friends, families, coworkers, etc., for fear of being harshly judged, laughed at, or both.

The good news, however, is that genuine interest in Witchcraft has been steadily on the rise for the last several decades, and is at an all-time high here in the Information Age.

The more people learn and understand what Witchcraft is (as well as what it isn't) the less stigma will be attached to this way of life and the people who follow it.

WHAT WITCHCRAFT
IS (AND ISN'T)

To help you get a better understanding of what witchcraft really is, let's take a closer look at the roots of Witchcraft, as well as clarifying a few common misconceptions.

ALL AROUND THE WORLD

In the broadest sense, the term "witchcraft" has been used by modern speakers of English to refer to an extremely wide range of beliefs, traditions and practices found in cultures across the globe and in every period of history since the dawn of humanity.

To use a random example, in ancient Mesopotamia, people wore amulets of ruby to guard against the "evil eye," while ancient Egyptians wore carnelian for the same purpose. And in the first century B.C., a Roman woman with the right skills could become a widely sought after source of healing and love potions.

These would all be considered examples of "witchcraft" from a modern, Judeo-Christian perspective, as would the shamanic healers among the !Kung people of Southern Africa, who have participated for centuries in trance dances in order to communicate with ancestral spirits to heal suffering among their communities.

In still another part of the world, Chinese homonyms (words that sound the same) take on identical symbolic meanings, adding a "superstitious" depth to the use of words and numbers in everyday life.

And in the U.S., many Mexican Americans in need of healing will seek out a *curandero*, a traditional healer who employs herbs, diet adjustments, and magic in his practice.

Each of these practices offers just a tiny glimpse of the very rich and complex world it is part of, and it's likely that none of the people mentioned here, regardless of the century they live(d) in, would ever call their way of life "witchcraft." They have (or *had*, in the case of our ancient friends) their own ways to name and describe their cultural traditions.

Nonetheless, "witchcraft" has often been used by speakers of English as a catch-all term for spiritual belief systems that have one or more of the following characteristics:

- They exist primarily outside of the world's dominant religions, such as Christianity, Islam, Judaism, Hinduism, etc.

- They involve a belief in phenomena that are disregarded by mainstream Western culture as either imaginary, "superstitious" or simply unexplainable by scientific means, such as an unseen "spirit world," paranormal activity, psychic abilities, magic, etc.

- They use resources from the natural world and the spirit world in the healing arts.

- They approach life from an animistic perspective, taking the view that everything on Earth, including inanimate objects, is alive.

As the above examples imply, these characteristics can be seen in belief systems all over the world and have been with us throughout our human history. Some cultures have kept their "native" spiritual traditions more or less intact for millennia—particularly in the East, where Christianity did not take over, displace, and/or stamp out indigenous practices.

The West, of course, is a different story.

While not *everything* in the pre-Christian Western world was destroyed by the rise and eventual dominance of "the Church," it's probably fair to say that most of the traditions and practices that we would now call "witchcraft" are lost to us.

Some traditions in specific areas—such as folk magic in rural parts of the British/Celtic Isles, for example—have managed to hang on over the centuries, but by and large there's been very little in the way of continuous practices that can be proven to predate the Christian Church.

As for Africa, Oceania, and the Americas, the extent to which indigenous beliefs and practices survived colonialism varies widely and depends largely on the level of brutality of the invaders of each area.

CLOSER TO HOME

Although a survey of indigenous practices across the globe would likely provide useful insights into the nature of spirituality and "occult" phenomena in general (including interesting similarities between geographically distant cultures), it would be well outside the scope of this guide.

Instead, the "witchcraft" discussed here has its roots in Europe, particularly in the British and Celtic Isles, and has spread in various forms over the last century to non-indigenous communities in North America, Australia, and New Zealand.

This is not to say that ideas, beliefs, etc. from other parts of the world haven't made their way into the "Western" Craft. Astrology, which informs much of contemporary Witchcraft, has its roots in the ancient Middle East, and the Hindu-Buddhist system of chakras also influences modern practices.

Indeed, as the innovations of humankind have made travel and the spread of information easier and easier over the course of millennia, the borders between cultural influences have become less firm than they may seem on the surface. And with the rise of globalization and the proliferation of the Internet, this is true today like never before.

Nonetheless, our focus here is on Witchcraft as it is practiced today in the Western Hemisphere, by those who actually identify their practice as Witchcraft (and perhaps a few who don't, but we'll get into the trickiness of terminology below).

For our purposes, it is spelled with a capital "W," to distinguish it from the generic "witchcraft" used by anthropologists and other academics to describe the wider range of practices around the world and throughout history.

A BRIEF HISTORY OF WESTERN "WITCHCRAFT"

Now that we've narrowed down our geographical understanding of what we mean when we talk about "Witchcraft," we can start to get closer to a working definition of what the Craft is all about.

If you look up "Witchcraft" on the Internet, using the phrase "Witchcraft is a..." you'll find a broad variety of words and phrases used to define it, such as "practice, spiritual practice, indigenous pre-Christian tradition, spiritual system, complex concept, a nature religion," etc.

But don't trust a standard dictionary to help you out in this regard! Most dictionary definitions oversimplify the word as being *merely* the practice of magic and/or "invoking spirits," and many emphasize associations with "black magic" or "evil spirits." (Whether or not any magic worked by a particular Witch is truly "black" is another matter, which will be discussed below.)

The issue here is that the popular notion of the word "witchcraft" is still under the spell of the legacy of Christian opposition to pagan practices. While some dictionaries are beginning to make reference to "Wicca" in these entries, we still have a long way to go before the centuries-old misconceptions about Witchcraft fade away.

In order to understand how the words "witch" and "witchcraft" (and even "pagan") became associated with the Judeo-Christian concept of "evil," it's helpful to review a little history. What follows is certainly not the whole story of the interaction between Christianity and Witchcraft (that alone could take several books to tell!), but can provide some historical context for the current, conflicting understandings of these words.

IN THE BEGINNING

Long before Christianity entered the picture, Europe, like the rest of the world, was full of many religions and belief systems, many of which included the practice of magic.

The first kind of spiritual belief system in human history is identified by anthropologists as "animism," the concept that spirits existed in what would appear to us to be non-living matter—rocks, rivers, etc., as well as plants and animals.

Pantheism, a related and sometimes co-existing concept, held that absolutely *everything* in the Universe was alive with divine consciousness. There was no division between the "sacred" and the "mundane," in the way most modern religions recognize. Instead, divinity existed everywhere—on Earth as well as in the heavens.

Eventually, out of these concepts grew polytheism, the concept that the various aspects of life involved in daily survival—available food, water, weather patterns, etc.—were governed by various deities.

By and large, these religions were "local"—different regions worshipped different local deities, and spiritual practitioners drew from their own communities' traditions, which might vary widely, depending on where they lived.

As people travelled and settled into new lands, however, some deities spread across vast territories. For example, Greek and Roman gods accompanied the Roman Empire throughout its reach, and certain Celtic gods of the British/Celtic Isles can be traced back to their origins in continental Europe.

Throughout these early centuries of "Western civilization," some cultures might build elaborate temples in which to worship their gods and goddesses, while others might simply make a pilgrimage to a spring where a particular deity was said to reside. But whatever form a particular region's religion might take, magic was a part of daily life, woven into the fabric of society through its role in spiritual and physical healing, and not considered to be separate from "ordinary reality."

When Christianity first began to spread throughout Roman-occupied Europe, missionaries had to contend with the gods and goddesses that people had been faithful to for centuries, and worked to convince people that Jesus was better than these older deities, with stronger magic.

This conversion happened more quickly in some places and more slowly in others, but it didn't happen overnight, and it wasn't accomplished strictly by force—despite the way the story is often told.

At first, many communities opted to integrate the story and message of Christianity into their own cosmologies, so that rather than replacing their deities and customs, Jesus and the rituals surrounding him existed side by side with the "old religion." The development of Irish Celtic Christianity is a good example of this type of integration of "pagan" and Christian culture.

But as the Church was determined to grow in power and influence, it became necessary to portray the old ways as being in line with "the Devil." This was a purely Judeo-Christian concept that had no correlation in the cosmologies of nature worshippers, but it came to define pagan beliefs and practices for centuries.

Speaking of "pagan," this is another word with multiple potential meanings and connotations.

Traced back to its origin in Latin, *paganus*, it simply meant a villager, or country dweller, as opposed to someone living in a city. Another meaning of this time period was "civilian," as in, a non-military person.

Once Christianity wormed its way into Latin, *paganus* came to mean someone who continued to worship the old gods and goddesses, and this gave rise to the word "heathen," meaning "one not enrolled in the army of Christ."

These days, "pagan" in the general sense simply refers to a person with religious beliefs that are not part of one of the dominant world religions.

Witchcraft is, therefore, considered a pagan religion, from an anthropological standpoint, though not all Witches will identify as "Pagans" with a capital "P." (Indeed, the range of options for labels and identities within the vast realm of contemporary "pagan" beliefs and practices is fairly dizzying and often confusing, and will be discussed in further detail, below.)

THE INVENTION OF "WITCHES"

It wasn't until Rome adopted Christianity as its official state religion in the late 4th century that pagan religions began to be systematically outlawed. And as the centuries wore on, the Church continued its battle to eradicate any and all competition for followers throughout Europe.

Seeking to discredit magic (which allowed people to participate in the shaping of their own lives and circumstances, rather than depending entirely on the new, all-powerful, singular deity), proponents of Christianity began to blame people who practiced magic for all kinds of misfortune—plagues, battles, weather disasters, etc.

Women in particular were scapegoated, as the male-dominated, patriarchal Church sought to take away the relatively high degree of power they had enjoyed in pre-Christian days.

As the Church's doctrine gradually took over the old religions, magic went underground, disappearing from everyday life, which made it even easier for those in power to convince people that magic was evil—after all, people are generally more afraid of what they don't understand.

And so, as magic became more shrouded in mystery and secrecy, it came to be seen as sinister.

So where does the word "witch" come in?

The etymology of this word is complicated, in that it can be traced back to Old English (spoken from around 400 to 1100 A.D.), but its origins before that are unclear.

Some linguists speculate that it arose out of older, pre-English Germanic words related to occult concepts, usually around divination practices. Rough translations of these older words include "sacred," "soothsayer," and "prophetic," as well as "to separate/divide" and "to make mysterious gestures." "To bend" is another educated guess, and this one shows up often in 20th and 21st century writing about the Craft, perhaps because it seems to relate to the power of Witches to "bend" reality to their will.

The truth is, no one really knows exactly how far back the origins of "witch" can be traced.

What we know for sure, however, is that the Old English version was "wicca," and it meant "sorcerer" or "diviner." (Technically, "wicca" was for males and "wicce" for females, but the gender distinction vanished by the time Middle English was in use, and "wicca" came to refer to both male and female. Incidentally, "wiccan" was the plural form of "wicca," which is not how the word is used today.)

The Anglo-Saxons who contributed this word to the ever-evolving English language would have made use of diviners in their pagan spiritual practices, and so it's fair to say that the roots of the word "witch" come from the days when a "witch" (i.e., a "wicca") was a perfectly acceptable thing to be.

However, by the time "wicca" morphed into "witch"—sometime during the 1500s—widespread persecution of pagan activity was well underway. So it's difficult to know whether the word had any positive (or even neutral) connotations at this point, or whether it had become completely negative.

Either way, as the witch-hunts in England reached their height during the 1600s, it was certainly not something anyone wanted to be called.

Scapegoating is always most easily accomplished when there's an easy, convenient word to use in order to whip up hysteria, and "witch" became just that word for a society increasingly afraid of its pagan past.

Women, and men, who continued to practice the old ways—or even just seemed like they might—were accused and convicted of "witchcraft," and subject to harsh punishment and even execution.

At certain times of particularly infectious hysteria, one could be accused of being a witch simply for having her own opinion or otherwise not "going with the crowd." It would be centuries until anyone in their right mind would choose to identify as a "witch," or be publicly associated with "witchcraft."

ENLIGHTENMENT AND REVIVAL

Although the Christians in power did their best to eradicate the old pagan ways throughout Europe over the centuries, all was not completely lost.

A few pockets of folk magic and folk healing practices remained more or less intact, in places like Cornwall, England and parts of Italy. And there had always been occult enthusists studying what they could and experimenting with what they had to work with.

From at least the 1200s and possibly earlier, and all the way up through to the 20th century, scholars of ancient mysticism and the like passed on their knowledge and experiences to future generations.

While possessing works by these authors may have been dangerous, depending on where you lived, clearly enough of their writing survived the assault on non-Christian ideas and practices. (In fact, some of modern Witchcraft's influences came through writers and philosophers who saw no conflict between Christianity and mysticism, and whose ideas were therefore more likely to be considered acceptable during these "religiously sensitive" years.)

So people with "pagan" or "witchy" leanings were certainly still present throughout the 1st and 2nd millennia, even if the old rituals and practices of deity-worship largely (or even completely) disappeared.

The hysteria over witches did eventually subside, as the Middle Ages gave way to the Enlightenment and the beginnings of modern science.

As more and more mysterious forces came to be explained in more rational, scientific ways, belief in witches and magic began to fade.

By the end of the 19th century, these beliefs, while still technically considered "heretical" in Christian society, were regarded more as a sign of ignorance than a moral failing.

This gradual shift in attitudes can be seen in the evolution of witchcraft laws in England, which went from treating witchcraft as a capital offense to barring people from claiming that anyone was even capable of such a practice. When the last Witchcraft Act (of 1735) was finally repealed (in 1951), it was because it seemed ridiculous to suggest, through legislation, that witchcraft existed in the first place.

Indeed, Western civilization's continual advances into the Industrial Age made fear of witchcraft seem downright silly. By the time the modern Witchcraft movement was getting underway, science and the modernization of the Western world had relegated the words "witch," "witchcraft" and "magic" to the world of fantasy (unless, of course, one was an occult enthusiast).

It was toward the middle of the 20th century that "witch" began to be claimed as a label by those who experimented with magic and other occult practices.

This was largely inspired by an academic theory, put forth by anthropologist Margaret Murray, that an ancient, pre-Christian "Witch-Cult" religion had spanned Europe, and had been practiced in secret until it was obliterated by the end of the Middle Ages.

Gerald Gardner, the primary founder of modern Wicca, was very taken with this theory, and began using the term "witchcraft" to describe the activities of himself and his fellow occultists.

He formed a coven, which he called "Bricket Wood," and referred to his fellow coveners as "the Wica," reviving the Old English word and giving it a plural, rather than singular, meaning (and an alternate spelling).

The "witch-cult" theory was later discredited due to lack of evidence. Regardless, now that it was no longer illegal to practice and/or speak of "witchcraft," these terms were reclaimed by a new generation of practitioners, and used with positive connotations—even with reverence and pride—for the first time in centuries.

SO IS WITCHCRAFT REALLY AN ANCIENT RELIGION?

One of the many commonly debated questions regarding Witchcraft today is whether it really is, as many of its practitioners say, an "ancient religion."

In order to properly examine this characterization, we first need to separate the words "ancient," and "religion."

Many people who identify as practitioners of Witchcraft will tell you that it's not a religion at all, while others maintain that it most certainly is. But before we tackle that tricky distinction, let's examine the "ancient" part, first.

If you read around on the subject of Witchcraft, particularly the Wiccan or Wiccan-inspired variety, you're likely to see more than a few statements claiming the practice to be an "old," "ancient," or even "prehistoric" tradition that was maintained in secret for centuries due to the religious and societal pressures described above.

Others will leave out the "ancient" part and only claim to trace their spiritual roots back to the Middle Ages, which is the period during which much of the written material that influences Witchcraft began to emerge.

Some Witches seem to like to give the appearance that everything in their personal practice was handed down over the centuries through a maternal line of "wise women," with each generation teaching the next, again, often in secret.

And while Wiccans will usually acknowledge the modern origins of their particular form of Witchcraft, including the fact that a good deal of the ritual material and ideas about deities were made up by Wicca's founders in the 20th century, the general belief among many is that these additions were divinely and authentically "gifted" to Gardner and other early pioneers, reclaimed from prior ages through spiritual means.

As we saw above, however, the practices and traditions that any modern Witchcraft is based on were all but eradicated by the first half of the last millennium. So those who claim to possess specific magical knowledge dating back "thousands of years" are not being literally truthful.

For one thing, written evidence in the form of spell instructions, ritual protocol, etc. is basically nonexistent—which is not surprising, given that the majority of the European population couldn't read or write. And in any case, as the persecution of witchcraft increased over time, having written evidence would have been very dangerous.

That's not to say that fragments of information haven't survived—in fact, the work of anthropologists, historians, and scientists in modern times has been very useful to those practitioners who are interested in being as faithful as possible to the old ways.

And the oral tradition can't be said to have entirely vanished, either—old ballads, myths, superstitions, bits of medicinal advice (some of which are now called "old wives' tales, others which continue to prove useful), and stories have clearly survived.

However, it's difficult to determine authenticity of much of this material, since it was recorded by monks and other outside observers, who would view it from a Christian standpoint, and often alter it as such, either out of a desire for censorship, or simply an unintentional effect of the melding of old and new religious culture.

There are other written sources of the theories, beliefs, and practices that can be found in modern Witchcraft, however. Writers of every century dating back to the dawn of the Middle Ages have recorded their own occult discoveries and documented those of others.

For example, a mystic living in the 13th century by the name of Moses de Leon wrote about his explorations of the esoteric teachings of the Jewish Kabbalah in a work called the Zohar. This work was studied by later students of the Kabbalah, and eventually came to influence leaders of the British occult revival of the late 1800s.

Two centuries after de Leon came Cornelius Agrippa, a scholar of European occult theories and traditions, including astrology, hermeticism, and other older belief systems from the ancient world. Agrippa's studies were collected in his *Three Books of Occult Philosophy*, which were also major contributors to what later came to be called the "Western Mystery Tradition."

The occult systems, beliefs, and traditions written about by earlier authors do not belong to Witchcraft per se. They represent distinct spiritual paths in their own right, and it's highly unlikely that many, if any of these authors would have identified as "witches."

But their theories, ideas, and adaptations of older belief systems influenced later spiritual scholars and thinkers, including—and perhaps most importantly in terms of modern Witchcraft—the British occult revivalists of the late 19th and early 20th centuries.

During this period of renewed interest in all things esoteric, figures like Helena Blavatsky, Samuel Mathers, and Aleister Crowley synthesized much of the ancient and medieval lore that came before them with their own mystical experiences, and contributed to many new occult movements and societies, like the Hermetic Order of the Golden Dawn, the religion of Thelema, and the Ordo Templi Orientis.

It was largely this group of philosophers and leaders that directly influenced the next generation of spiritual pioneers—namely, the first "Wiccans" of the 20th century.

For better or for worse, the "ancient lineage" idea as it persists in the 21st century can be largely attributed to these early leaders of what later came to be called Wicca.

Gerald Gardner, for his part, claimed to have been initiated into his version of the Craft through participation in a coven practicing in the New Forest area of England.

This coven was said to be a surviving remnant of the "Witch-Cult" religion theorized by Margaret Murray, and while Gardner never provided much specific information about his experiences with the coven, he did attribute the majority of the beliefs and practices he brought to his own Bricket Wood coven to these New Forest Witches.

Historians have debated whether this New Forest coven ever existed, but those who argue that it did acknowledge that it was not, in fact, a direct continuation of a specific ancient religion.

Furthermore, Gardner eventually admitted that he had borrowed much of the material in his Book of Shadows for Bricket Wood from other existing sources—such as medieval occult texts, the works of Aleister Crowley, and the rituals of contemporary magical societies.

Following Gardner was Alex Sanders, the founder of Alexandrian Wicca, who also maintained the premise that his traditions and practices were ancient when he had, in fact, mostly made them up.

According to other Witches who were part of his circle, Sanders particularly enjoyed telling all kinds of stories about the ancient lineage of "British Traditional Witchcraft" to gullible Americans, who returned to the States and cultivated the myth, where it continues to thrive to this day.

But it wasn't only those who came to be called "Wiccan" who were guilty of telling tall tales. Robert Cochrane, founder of a divergent branch of Witchcraft now known as Cochrane's Craft, insisted that he was descended from a family of Witches going back to the 1600s, a claim that was later debunked.

Although it's unfortunate that some individuals involved in the origins of modern Witchcraft felt the need to resort to such fabrications, it doesn't diminish the authenticity of the spiritual path followed by adherents to Wicca and other forms of "Traditional" Witchcraft. No one can measure the age of the wisdom, power, and beauty found in these forms of interaction with the spiritual world.

For those practicing the Craft today, it can seem very understandable that Murray's theory of a continuous and widespread "Witch-Cult" would have been a powerful and enchanting idea.

In fact, many Witches to this day feel themselves to have "inherited" the call to their practice in some form or other. Some even believe they are reincarnations of former Witches who were unable to safely practice their Craft in previous lives due to persecution.

It may be that this feeling of "ancient lineage" is simply part of the human psyche's relationship to the divine, and that those founders who claimed a literal history that doesn't exist were just responding to that sense of timeless connection—which certainly exists on the spiritual plane.

So as far as the "lineage" of modern Witchcraft is concerned, it's fair to conclude that it draws from a blend of traditions.

This includes European folk customs as well as other belief systems with roots that predate the modern era—such as astrology, Tarot and other divination systems, older esoteric traditions like Hermeticism and Kabbalah, and other ancient forms of mysticism. Added to this blend are influences from more recent traditions, such as the occult societies of the late 19th and early 20th centuries mentioned above, and even more recent developments of the middle and late 20th century.

It's also fair to say that for many, Witchcraft is a continually evolving spectrum of practices that emerge as new generations of Witches forge their own paths, drawing from the vast well of older systems and adapting and adding to them based on their own experiences.

Given that this is exactly what occultists have been doing since our first known sources of esoteric traditions, it could be argued that diverging from the "ancient path" is a way of continuing that very same path.

Furthermore, we can think of religions and belief systems in general as dynamic, continually evolving, and influencing one other. For example, the Roman pantheon of deities borrows heavily from the earlier Greek system.

There are also interesting similarities in the genesis myths of many different Native American societies, and a study of Celtic history will show how particular Celtic gods spread across Europe as these tribes grew in territory and influence.

The Kabbalah tradition has spread into other religions from its native Judaism, which also gave birth, of course, to Christianity.

So although today's Witches and other Pagans are following paths that are technically new—and often flat-out inventing their own practices—they echo and pay homage to old forms.

There's no reason to suppose that a deity like the Greek Zeus couldn't still be influencing believers today, if they choose to allow that, just as Brighid (or Brigh) never completely disappeared from Irish culture. To bring these old ways back in whatever form we're able to understand now is to perpetuate them into the present and the future.

Therefore, the phenomenon we know as Witchcraft is both ancient and brand-new. It's a paradox that some might find difficult to comprehend or accept, but in the timeless quality of the larger Universe, it really doesn't matter.

As for whether or not "religion" is an appropriate word for Witchcraft, it really tends to be up to the individual practitioner's definition of the word.

For some people, "religion" calls up images of churches, temples, or other formal places of worship that belong to organized institutions—particularly Judaism, Christianity, and/or Islam.

Those who were brought up in religions they no longer feel connected to before coming to Witchcraft tend not to feel comfortable describing their Craft as a religion. Others, noting the considerable amount of social and military conflict throughout history in the name of one religion or other, are strongly against the idea of being thought to belong to any religion.

Many people these days—Witches and non-Witches alike—prefer the word "spiritual" to "religious," in order to distance themselves from what they perceive to be dogmatic, inflexible, and even intolerant modes of thinking.

"Spiritual" people, in this view, are free to explore and decide for themselves what they believe, while "religious" people believe what they're told to believe by their religious leaders, with no room for their own personal observations or experiences.

Religion is most generically defined as a particular system of faith and worship involving a power that is greater than humanity. Usually this "power" takes the form of one or more deities.

Whether this applies to Witchcraft is debatable, as not all Witches believe in specific deities—they may simply acknowledge that nature in itself is the "power" greater than humanity, without needing to name any aspect of it.

Wicca, however, is a form of Witchcraft that does have deities at its core, and is generally recognized as a religion in the United States and elsewhere, even if it isn't thought of in the same way as the dominant monotheistic religions. But Witchcraft, with its infinite variety of pathways and practices, and its allowance for deities and absence of deities, seems less of a religion and more of a looser set of beliefs and practices.

Some Witches do define Witchcraft as a religion. Others absolutely reject the term. Some Witches identify as atheists, while others consider themselves to be agnostic. Still others both practice Witchcraft *and* belong to a formal religion like Christianity or Judaism, blending elements of each tradition into their own belief system.

Indeed, the flexibility of Witchcraft as a way of life allows for limitless possibilities when it comes to how its practitioners identify and describe their own paths.

The truth is that it doesn't matter whether you consider Witchcraft to be a "religion," because there will never be a single "authority" within the Craft who can (or would want to) make that call.

A FEW MODERN MISCONCEPTIONS

Clearly, there are questions about Witchcraft that don't have easy answers. As stated elsewhere in this guide, Witchcraft may be easier to define in terms of what it isn't, than in terms of what it is.

Before moving on to a more detailed discussion of the many different schools and forms of Witchcraft, let's look at a few common misunderstandings that, despite the Information Age, still persist in mainstream culture.

Witchcraft is not the same as sorcery, as mainstream culture tends to understand the word.

While "sorcery" is often used as a synonym for "witchcraft," its connotations tend to bring up images of long-bearded wizards in tall, conical hats creating thunderstorms and summoning dragons to attack their enemies.

These terms may have been interchangeable in the past, and perhaps still are in the world of fantasy, but there are many practicing Witches in the real world who would not describe what they do as sorcery.

The ethos of Witchcraft is one of *working with* the natural forces of the world, rather than *commanding* them.

Most Witches only work for results that do no harm to others, as is seen in a very common closing refrain in spellwork: "for the good of all, and harm to none." Others consider the intention of their work as strictly neutral, with neither positive nor negative implications.

Of course, it can't be denied that there are some who freely utilize their skills to manipulate the behavior of others or even cause them harm, and some of these people do embrace the term "sorcerer." (Some may also identify as Witches, but most Witches won't thank them for it.)

At any rate, "sorcery" tends to suggest either make-believe, unnecessary ego, or ill intentions—and possibly all three.

Witchcraft is also not the same as ceremonial magic, although there may be some overlap in the practices of these two traditions.

Ceremonial magic came about as a result of the renewed interest in the occult in England in the mid-19th century. It generally involves elaborate, highly formalized rituals (it is sometimes called "high magic") which are kept secret by the initiated members of a specific organized group.

Its practices are not so much rooted in the natural world, but rather rely heavily on symbolism and man-made objects (cups, swords, elaborate costumes, etc.)

Some Witches, particularly those practicing in covens, may follow rituals with a degree of complexity that is similar to ceremonial magic, but many are far less formal in their magical work, and may just as soon design a ritual "on the spot" if they feel inspired to do so.

Finally, Witchcraft is, of course, not Satanism or "devil-worship."

This is probably the most long-standing and widespread misconception about the Craft, perpetuated by Christian propaganda dating back to the time of the Roman Empire.

Even today, the Internet is full of websites from all branches of Christianity—even fairly "enlightened" denominations—claiming that Witchcraft is based on some sort of "pact" with "the devil" or an "evil spirit."

First, "Satan" as a tempter to evil deeds in Christianity is a concept that never existed in the pagan world.

Second, as a historical deity, "Satan" actually predates the Bible, so those who do pay attention to him today are not worshipping the Biblical figure.

Generally speaking, those who identify as Satanists do not actually tend to be proponents of "evil" or causing harm to others. In some traditions, Satan is actually a benevolent figure.

Still, the name simply can't help but suggest otherwise, and for this reason many (even most) Witches keep their distance from the name and the term. There have been Satanists who also claim to be under the Witchcraft umbrella, but it's more accurate to place them under the larger umbrella of "Pagan."

At any rate, without getting into the nuances of individual ritual practices and how they may or may not include some concept of a deity called "Satan," this guide is not including such practices in the definition of Witchcraft.

A DIVERSITY OF PATHS

So far, we've identified some essential characteristics of Witchcraft as it fits within the larger context of pagan belief systems around the globe, and taken a brief look at the origins of Witchcraft in Western Europe. We've also examined some of the main myths and misconceptions that surround this dynamic and versatile realm of spirituality.

In Part Two, we'll look more closely at several different forms of practice that exist collectively under the umbrella term of "Witchcraft," and highlight important distinctions between a few of these forms.

If you're new to Witchcraft and wondering where to begin exploring options for your own personal practice, this next section can help you gain a better sense of what might resonate best with you.

Pay attention to your intuition as you read—any passages that cause you to feel a certain inner "tug" are likely helping to guide you in the right direction!

PART TWO

FORMS OF CONTEMPORARY WITCHCRAFT

BRANCHES OF THE CRAFT

It's probably obvious to you by now that Witchcraft is a practice that defies easy definitions. This was likely always the case, but it's especially so in these days of the Internet Age.

As interest in the Craft has increased exponentially over the past couple of decades, an amazing variety of forms and traditions has been coming out of the woodwork, and new ones are being created as well.

Indeed, the speed with which the awareness, knowledge, and development of Witchcraft has been growing is almost overwhelming. Even if it were possible to identify and describe each and every different "branch" of the Craft as it exists today, it's likely a new form or two would emerge before such a catalogue came off the presses. (Of course, it could never be possible to account for every single form of Witchcraft, since there's no way to account for every Witch.)

Nonetheless, it is possible to draw some basic distinctions between a few main "limbs" of the tree of the Craft, while acknowledging that one's personal practice may fit neatly into one category, or include elements from more than one.

PAGANISM: THE UMBRELLA'S UMBRELLA

One often confusing aspect of the terminology around Witchcraft is the use of the words "pagan," "Pagan" and "NeoPagan."

Before delving into the different forms of Witchcraft as it's practiced today, it's useful to take a look at these terms—particularly because many authors on the topic tend to use one or more of them to describe the Craft—and may even use them interchangeably with "Witch" or even "Wiccan."

As discussed earlier in this guide, the classic, or academic definition of "pagan" relates to any religious belief or tradition that does not belong to one of the world's dominant, monotheistic religions.

In this sense, everything but Christianity, Judaism, and Islam is essentially pagan.

However, the "pagan" was initially developed in relation to Western religions, so it really applied to those who worshipped or honored local deities in the Western hemisphere, as opposed to Buddhists or Hindus, for example.

These days, you'll find the capitalized "Pagan" used to identify a broad variety of spiritual and/or religious traditions in the West, of which Witchcraft is just one.

Indeed, if "Witchcraft" is an umbrella term for a set of beliefs and practices that share a fair amount of similarities, "Paganism" is an even larger umbrella, encompassing movements like modern Druidism, shamanism, various types of goddess-worship, and plenty of other occult practices that aren't considered Witchcraft.

Many, but not all, Pagan traditions incorporate polytheism (the belief in more than one deity), an animistic view of the world, and a sense of the afterlife.

Some Pagans are eclectic practitioners of a variety of traditions with various old or new origins, while others are reconstructionist—they only follow practices that are known to have existed in former centuries and strive to be as faithful to history as possible. Some of these traditions involve the practice of magic, but not all.

Many Witches acknowledge this connection with the larger Pagan community, but some do not. This is also true of other forms—practitioners of modern Druidism, for example, might reject the term "Pagan," even though their beliefs and activities fall perfectly within the general use of the term.

(As for "NeoPagan," this is used by some in order to acknowledge the difference between modern Pagans and the pagans of old, who obviously lived very different lives and would have had very different practices. Others prefer "contemporary Pagan" instead, since "Neo" almost seems to imply that there isn't anything authentic about their practices.)

At any rate, the umbrella term of "Paganism" can be helpful in understanding how seemingly very different traditions, beliefs, and practices can sit side by side in a larger grouping. It's within this larger context that this guide views the many different forms of Witchcraft, and we'll focus specifically now on three fairly broad categories: Traditional Witchcraft, Wicca, and contemporary Witchcraft.

THE MANY DEFINITIONS OF "TRADITIONAL WITCHCRAFT"

If you look up "Traditional Witchcraft" on the Internet, you are certain to end up with a wide range of conflicting definitions, explanations, and philosophies.

Depending on which sites you read, you're also fairly likely to come across some animosity expressed by some site authors and/or commenters—sometimes toward Wiccans, and other times toward other Witches whose understanding of "Traditional" doesn't match their own.

In fact, just about any single definition or description of "Traditional Witchcraft" with a capital "T" has a good chance of seeming incorrect or even controversial to one Witch or another. These disagreements can arise out of geographical and cultural differences, as well as the extent to which the verifiable history of the tradition in question—in the sense of existing academic knowledge—matters to the individual practitioner.

Since people from many differing forms of Witchcraft claim to be "Traditional" Witches, there's probably never going to be consensus on what is and isn't "Traditional Witchcraft."

In a way, it would be impossible to point with any certainty to who or what is the most "traditional" in a spiritual practice with origins as varied and admittedly murky as what we have come to call "Witchcraft."

At any rate, it seems that the more the Craft grows, adapts, and takes on new forms, the more there are practitioners who don't care for the changes, and therefore identify with the word "Traditional" in order to distinguish their own practice from that of the "newcomers."

By and large, the popularity and growth of Wicca in particular has been a chief catalyst for many non-Wiccan Witches seeking refuge in the "Traditional" label.

However, "Traditional" can also apply to anyone following a previously established *tradition* of the Craft, as opposed to following an "eclectic" path created and/or adapted from various traditions.

In this sense of the word, someone practicing Traditional Gardnerian Wicca would also identify as a Traditional Witch, even though others might call this person a Traditional Wiccan.

In an attempt to make at least a few clear distinctions out of the dizzying array of forms of Witchcraft in the 21st century, this guide will treat all forms of Wicca as being separate from Traditional Witchcraft, while acknowledging that there may be overlapping practices between the two.

Below, we'll survey the particular elements of Wicca that make it "non-traditional" in comparison to other forms, but first we'll identify two broad categories of Witchcraft that are generally considered to fall under the "Traditional" umbrella.

1. TRADITIONAL WITCHCRAFT

The first category of Traditional Witchcraft covers anyone whose practice is rooted in a tradition known to date back at least before the 20th century, and is *not* influenced by the ideas or practices that came out of the English occult revival of the late 19th century.

This distinction is made in order to identify traditions that are native to specific regions and cultures, rather than those created from a variety of sources, places and time periods.

Practitioners in this category include folk healers, those known as "hereditary witches," and reconstructionists.

Many of the traditions that make up this category are thought to have roots in pre-Christian times. However, since Christianity gradually infiltrated all of Europe, records of these traditions are likely to have a Christian imprint. (As they say, "history is written by the victors.")

Actually, depending on the place and time period, it was entirely possible to be a Christian *and* practice some form of "the old religion," especially when it came to folk healing and folk magic. So any influences of or references to Christianity that may be found within past or present forms of the traditions mentioned here are by no means a reason to consider any of these practices inauthentically "traditional."

It should also be mentioned that many practitioners in this category do not identify (and never did identify) as "Witches."

In many of these traditions, which were actually around during the time of the witch hunts, the word "witch" was indeed an insult at best.

At worst, it was a serious charge that could get one in very deep trouble.

One historical name, still used by some who practice the form in England, is "cunning folk," which we will take a closer look at below. Another widely preferred alternative term used today is "Traditional Crafter," which puts the emphasis on the path, or "craft," one follows, without any need to rely on the "'W' word."

Nonetheless, this guide includes these older practices in the umbrella term of "Witchcraft," for two reasons.

First, the practices themselves fall very clearly into the *anthropological* sense of the word "witchcraft," discussed at the beginning of Part One.

Second, many of these individual practices—whether it's magic spells, myth and lore, spiritual beliefs, or healing methods—have been absorbed into the larger traditions of those who do identify as Witches, and are therefore now part of "Witchcraft" in the 21st century.

FOLK HEALERS

Probably the most well-documented practice of what we now consider to be part of Traditional Witchcraft is that of the folk healer.

Records dating back to at least the 15th century show folk healers operating throughout Christianized Europe, with each country, region, and even county having their own specific folklore traditions.

Fragments of many of these traditions have indeed been passed down to us, often in the form of what we now call "old wives' tales" or "superstitions," but in some places, particularly in rural areas of Britain and Ireland, these traditions have remained surprisingly intact as they've lived on through the centuries.

Of course, the term "folk healer" doesn't quite accurately describe what these people were (and are) capable of.

In addition to attending to medical problems, folk healers practiced magic and divination—and might indeed use magic and divination as part of their healing techniques.

You could almost think of them as the "holistic" healers of their time, going beyond the physical or biological level and into the spiritual realms in order to identify and solve the underlying problems of their clients.

These practitioners had different names in different areas of Europe. They were called *benandanti* in Italy ("good walkers") and *klok gumma* or *klok gubbe* in Swedish ("wise old woman" or "wise old man"). In England, they were called "cunning folk," which, as mentioned above, is a term still in use among some who still practice these healing and magical arts.

Cunning folk provided a variety of services to their communities, including herbal remedies, healing charms and potions, divination services, love magic, locating lost items, and a host of other magical means of solving their clients' problems.

Interestingly, cunning folk often provided the antidotes for "evil spells" cast by "witches." So strong was the belief in malicious witchcraft in these times that people could be easily convinced that any misfortune that befell them was the deliberate act of a witch.

In fact, historians argue that without this belief, there would have been no business for the cunning folk. This is part of why the term "witch" isn't seen to be accurate for cunning folk, though they were sometimes referred to as "white witches" to distinguish their magic from the malevolent kind.

However, it has been pointed out that some cunning folk had no problem performing curses or hexes for money, while others might actually secretly curse or hex a potential client, who would then come to them for a cure!

This is likely to seem highly unethical to most modern readers, but for people trying to make a living in hard times, and in a culture so full of belief in negative magic, it likely seemed relatively harmless, if not very honest.

One important characteristic of traditional folk magic is its integral relationship with the physical landscape it grew out of. For example, a given spell or remedy will only use ingredients from the plant and animal life found in the region where the tradition occurs.

A folk healer in England would never have used hibiscus in any magical workings, as it couldn't be found anywhere nearby. Likewise, a ritual remedy involving water from a specific stream or river would be tied to a legend associated with that body of water, so the ritual significance wouldn't "translate" if exported to some other part of the world.

Another aspect to note is that folk magic was not inherently religious or even "spiritual"—as previously mentioned, the religion of most folk healers was Christianity.

While some of these practitioners did work with spirits as part of their magic, they did not worship pagan deities and would probably not have conducted rituals other than for specific purposes, such as breaking a curse. (Those who did incorporate religion into their practice were predominantly Roman Catholics, particularly in Italy, who would petition the saints for assistance in their workings.)

Many who practice folk magic today see it as an art, which may be incorporated by some into a larger religious or spiritual practice, but which in and of itself is not at all religious.

It is thought by most scholars that the cunning craft "died out" as a profession sometime in the middle of the 20th century, declining steadily as populations became more literate and educated and left their beliefs in malevolent witchcraft behind.

However, many of the magical spells, charms, remedies, etc. used by the cunning folk have been absorbed into the practices of contemporary magicians and healers, both those who identify as Witches and those who still prefer the "cunning" title.

Individuals practicing folk magic today may follow the traditions of a specific region, or combine practices from differing places, depending on preference and/or the availability of information.

A few specific traditions of folk m
particularly well-preserved in pr
well as areas of the southern Un.
traditions combined with elements c
form "Hoodoo," a magical healing sy>
some in the Appalachian mountains.

children born
recent origi
In som
descend
several
intere
who
the

HEREDITARY WITC

Compared to folk magic, there is very little in the wo,
documentation for what is called "Hereditary Witchcraft," .
passing down of very old traditions from one generation in a
the next.

This is largely because such families, which are believed to be qui.
rare, keep their traditions to themselves and don't publish books or
build websites devoted to their Craft.

This secrecy is most likely a leftover effect of Christianity's near-total
devastation of the "old ways" that eventually became part of the
tradition itself, but whatever the case, these traditions are highly
personal and the practices are not shared with outsiders.

Another name for this form of the Craft is Family Traditionalism, or
"Fam Trad," which emphasizes the point.

It could almost be likened to a grandmother's "secret recipe" for a
casserole that's been passed down through generations, only the
recipe would never be shared with dinner guests, no matter how close
the friendships might be.

Hereditary Witchcraft in this classic sense may include folk magic
and shamanic practices, and could involve deities as well, particularly
those that hung on (however partially) through the Christianization of
Europe, although working with spirits of the land around the family's
traditional home would be more likely. Again, it's hard to point to any
specific examples due to the closed nature of these traditions.

Another way to view the definition of "hereditary," however, is *any*
tradition that is handed down through family members, so that

to Wiccans and other Witches of traditions with more
s can also be considered hereditary Witches.

cases, the inheritor of the tradition may not be a direct
nt of the person handing it down, and it can definitely skip
generations before it is reclaimed—usually only partially—by
ted descendants of the tradition. This is particularly true of those
come from regions where folk magic has only begun to wane in
ast two generations or so.

Finally, there are those with more "neo-Pagan" or "neo-Witchcraft"
eanings who consider initiation into a coven to be a form of hereditary
Craft, but this is symbolically hereditary rather than literally so.

RECONSTRUCTIONISTS

In the contemporary Pagan world, several movements have cropped
up that strive to emulate the pre-Christian practices of various ancient
cultures—particularly the Greek, Roman, Norse, Germanic, and Celtic
peoples.

Followers of these movements strive to be as historically accurate as
possible, with the aim of reviving these traditions as they actually were,
rather than creating new traditions "inspired" by them.

They use research from the fields of anthropology and history, study
the ancient mythology, and worship the deities of their chosen
tradition's pantheons.

Most reconstructionists, or "recons" as they are often called, do not
practice magic and do not identify as Witches. However, a form of
reconstructionist Witchcraft does exist, often borrowing from the same
sources and staying faithful to what is known, with little to no invention
of details to fill in the gaps.

Reconstructionist Witches are likely to be eclectic in their practice,
using spells and other workings from more than one tradition, as
opposed to sticking with a single region or culture.

Unlike folk healers and hereditary practitioners, there's no real case
to be made for a continuous handing-down of the tradition—

reconstructionists may have little to no actual familial or geographical connection to the traditions they study and practice.

However, they are included in this first category of Traditional Witchcraft because they don't incorporate ideas, beliefs, or other traditions associated with the "modern" forms of Witchcraft springing from the English occult revival of the late 19th century.

2. TRADITIONALIST WITCHCRAFT

As you may have guessed, this category *does* include those forms of the Craft that incorporate practices developed during, or inspired by, the English occult revival.

The reason this movement is so important to understanding what various practitioners may or may not mean by "Traditional" is that an enormous amount of what is considered the basis of modern Witchcraft was rediscovered and/or developed during this time period.

As discussed in Part One, there were several ancient occult belief systems and practices— like the Kabbalah, astrology, and hermeticism—that continued to fascinate occultists of the Middle Ages. Their writings and new adaptations, including specifically Western additions such as the Tarot and ceremonial magic, were then revived and built upon by occultists of the late 19th century in England.

These revivalists continued to develop ceremonial magic and other esoteric beliefs and practices that fall under the umbrella term of "Western Mystery Tradition," forming occult societies such as the Hermetic Order of the Golden Dawn.

Although some folk healers practiced astrology, and some took an interest in ceremonial magic as it became popular in England, the activities of the occult revivalists generally had little or no connection to their traditional practices, which is why much of what stems from this period isn't considered to be true "Traditional Craft" by some.

However, astrology, ceremonial magic, the Tarot system of divination, etc. certainly qualify as "traditions" in their own right, as they date back several centuries, and have been incorporated into many forms of what we now call Witchcraft for several generations.

The influences of the English occult revival—as well as other such revivals in various parts of Europe dating back to the 18th century—were still obviously in play in the early and middle decades of the 1900s, which is when the many forms of the second kind of Traditional Witchcraft have their modern beginnings.

It's in this period that practitioners and proponents of what increasingly came to be called Witchcraft started forming covens, exchanging ideas, and writing about their experiences.

Not everyone involved in the Craft at this point wanted to be public about it, but some—especially Gerald Gardner—-were all for sharing as much information as possible in order to keep their "old religion" from disappearing again. In this, Gardner and others were highly successful, as their form of Witchcraft spread from Britain to America and beyond.

By the mid-1960s, America was having its own sort of occult revival, and what was now being increasingly called "Wicca" was received enthusiastically by many different types of spiritual seekers. And America, being the "melting pot" that it is, was a place where the British "traditions" were adopted, adapted, and interwoven with other influences to create several new forms of Witchcraft, all with varying degrees of similarity to what we now call "Gardnerian Wicca."

There are too many forms of this second category of Traditional Witchcraft—on both sides of the pond—to discuss in this introductory guide, and there are certainly bound to be forms and traditions that operate in total secrecy.

However, a few recognized forms stand out as being fairly prominent, and at least somewhat accessible to outsiders, either through access to a coven, an individual teacher, or through information in print and online. These forms, or "paths," include the British Cochrane's Craft and Sabbatic Craft, and the American-born Feri, 1734, and Stregheria traditions.

With the exception of Sabbatic Craft, these forms have been around for at least three decades, if not longer, and are all based on older traditions.

While some authors on the topic of Witchcraft will include one or more of these forms in the category of Wicca, it is highly unlikely that most people practicing one of these forms would agree—the majority prefer the term Traditional Witchcraft.

Some in this category may also prefer "Traditional Crafter" to describe themselves, rather than "Traditional Witch," but by and large, the "W" word is not a problem for these practitioners.

THE FERI TRADITION

The Feri Tradition is one of the few modern forms of Traditional Craft that has identifiable roots which predate Wicca. In other words, the primary founders of the tradition—Victor Anderson and his wife, Cora—were involved in Witchcraft before coming across any of Gardner's writings.

From a fairly young age, Victor Anderson had encountered magical traditions and practices through acquaintance with several practitioners, including members of a coven called "the Harpy Coven," which he joined in 1932.

Cora came from a Witchcrafting family in the South and was reputed to have excellent magical skills in the kitchen.

The couple lived and practiced on the West Coast of the United States, simply referring to their practice as "Witchcraft" or "The Craft" and initiating others into it from the mid-1940s onward.

It wasn't until Witchcraft was really on the rise, in the 1960s, that the group began to refer to it as the "Feri Tradition" in order to distinguish their practice from the increasingly diverse array of other forms. This particular spelling, "Feri," came later, as more and more NeoPagan groups began to use "faerie" or "fairy" in association with their own practices.

Despite the name's connection with Celtic spiritual lore, the Feri Tradition is not particularly "Celtic" in essence. Its influences are very wide-reaching, with roots in Vodou and Hoodoo—traditional forms of Witchcraft found in the U.S.—as well as the Western esoteric paths of Gnosticism and Kabbalah, the Eastern tradition of Tantra, and Huna, another "New Age" system very loosely based on indigenous Hawaiian religion.

Feri has its own distinct pantheon of deities as well as unique symbology and practices that, while they may be borrowed from other spiritual paths, are not found outside of this Tradition.

This path is lineage-based, meaning that you cannot really learn it on your own, but need to seek out a teacher who is already an initiate of Feri. It isn't necessary to join a coven, however—in fact, solitary practice is quite common among followers of the Feri path.

Anderson did, of course, encounter Gardner's writings in the mid-1950s, and was said to be inspired by them to take on new initiates and spread the Tradition more deliberately. However, there's very little similarity between Gardnerian Wicca and the Feri Tradition.

COCHRANE'S CRAFT

Cochrane's Craft, also referred to as "Cochrane-based Witchcraft" and sometimes "Cochranianism," is a Tradition based on the work and teachings of Robert Cochrane (whose real name was Roy Bowers).

Cochrane was one of the many Witches working in Britain in the mid-20th century, and he was acquainted with many of the same people that Gerald Gardner worked with in his coven.

Cochrane disliked Gardner and many of his specific practices, however, and is actually the person who coined the term "Gardnerian," which later, of course, became the official name for Gardner's form of Witchcraft.

Cochrane formed his own coven, called the Clan of Tubal Cain, in the early 1960s.

He claimed to be a Hereditary Witch, descended from a family of Witches going back several centuries, but family members later denied this.

Nonetheless, his approach to the Craft was highly influential to many Witches, particularly those who didn't resonate with the Gardnerian form. He was said to have a closer connection to nature, and to be more interested in mysticism than Gardner and his fellow Witches, who were more focused on ritual and magic.

Interestingly, one of Cochrane's chief contributions to 20th-century Witchcraft was the belief in a "triple goddess," which was inspired by the writer Robert Graves and his book, *The White Goddess: a Historical Grammar of Poetic Myth.*

This concept of deity, as we will see later, has become a central part of modern Wiccan cosmology.

Other elements of Cochrane's approach centered on his preference for spontaneous rituals, rather than pre-planned ceremonies with written instructions, and a more shamanic style of interaction with the spirit world.

His influence has lived on in many forms, including the continuation of the Clan of Tubal Cain, newer Traditions inspired by Cochrane's teachings, and plenty of solitary practitioners around the globe.

1734

1734 is a North American Tradition directly inspired by Cochrane's work, in that its principal founder, Joe Wilson, was in correspondence with Cochrane for the last year of Cochrane's life and based this new Tradition on those letters, along with the teachings of two other Witches who were influential to him.

Wilson was adamant that 1734 was not a lineage-based system and that it had no true leaders. Therefore, there is no "initiation" into the Tradition, although for those who find initiation to be important, there are groups within 1734 that will honor it.

There are also offshoots of the Tradition that that identify as Wiccan, though similarities between 1734 and most mainstream Wicca are fairly superficial. Like Cochrane's original practice, 1734 is more about mysticism than celebratory ritual.

The ritual similarities that do exist are more due to the lack of original material to follow—Cochrane wrote no books and never left written instructions—than anything else.

As for the name, "1734" is said to be a grouping of numbers that has significance to Witches. It is a riddle of sorts, and it's said that solving the riddle will reveal the name of the Goddess.

STREGHERIA

Stregheria is an Italian-American form of Witchcraft based in the practices of Italian immigrants to America who drew from centuries-old Etruscan traditions.

It was initially brought to light by Leo Martello, an Italian-American self-proclaimed Hereditary who wrote about it in *Witchcraft: The Old Religion* in the early 1970s.

The name "Stregheria" was introduced in the mid-1990s by Raven Grimassi, another Witch claiming to have inherited his practice from earlier generations, who founded two Traditions within the form.

The Aridian Tradition was a solitary practice based on self-dedication to the Craft, while the Arician Tradition involves a rite of initiation.

Being an essentially American-born Tradition, Stregheria has acquired elements that borrow from Wiccan forms, but its deities and rituals are culturally rooted in the area of Europe now known as Italy.

This path is open to all—one does not have to be of Italian descent to explore and practice Stregheria.

SABBATIC CRAFT

Sabbatic Craft is a term coined by Andrew Chumbley, a British occultist, magician, and prolific author who was Magister of a British magical group called the Cultus Sabbati.

Chumbley was an inheritor of two different lines of Witchcraft in England and Wales, which predated the revivalist movement that led to Wicca. Although he was primarily rooted in East Anglian forms of Traditional Craft, he also had intense interest in other occult areas, including ceremonial magic and direct interaction with the spiritual world.

He believed that all magic came from the same source, though he had his own distinct vocabulary to describe the beliefs and practices of his Tradition.

"Sabbatic Craft" and "Sabbatical Witchcraft" are terms used by Witches and other magicians who follow Chumbley's beliefs and practices, but are not members of Cultus Sabbati.

This is not an initiatory path of Witchcraft, but it's also not very accessible to those new to the world of the occult. Newcomers are advised to read widely in the area of the Western Mystery Tradition in order to better understand Chumbley's work.

Incidentally, Chumbley did use the word "sorcery" to refer to his magic, but also called it the "nameless arte," as it was often referred to in the East Anglian Tradition.

Chumbley did most of his writing in the 1990s, and died in 2004 at age 37, meaning that while the material this path of the Craft is based on is quite old, Sabbatic Craft itself is the youngest of this group of "Traditional" forms of Witchcraft.

MODERN "TRADITIONS"

By now you'll have noticed that although the paths described above are called "Traditional," none of them are actually older than the 20th century.

In this sense, they are every bit as "modern" as Wicca, the form that most Traditionalists are trying to distinguish themselves from by using the term "Traditional."

Furthermore, each of these Traditions is its own sort of hybrid, combining elements from disparate sources and (usually) allowing for new adaptations to emerge, which is more or less how Wicca was formed. (And to make things even more confusing, there are people who identify as British Traditional Witches who actually follow Gardner's form of Witchcraft very strictly, but don't use the word "Wicca" because Gardner did not.)

Nonetheless, those who identify as Traditional Witches (or Traditional Crafters, as some prefer) are, by and large, not Wiccans.

DISTINGUISHING "WICCA" FROM "TRADITIONAL" AND "WICCAN" FROM "WITCH"

So why all the fuss about distinctions, anyway? Why is there so much debate and seeming need to either align with or distance oneself from "Wicca"?

The answer to this rather depends on who you are and where you're coming to the Craft from, but there tend to be a couple of main reasons.

"New" Witches—those just discovering the Craft for the first time—are likely to encounter Wicca first, since the vast majority of available print and online resources regarding the Craft are primarily Wiccan in origin. (In fact, it could be argued that Wicca is the main reason anyone in this century knows anything about modern Witchcraft!)

Some of these newcomers will stay on the Wiccan path, while others find they don't resonate with what it has to offer.

They may still want to explore Witchcraft, just not as a Wiccan. Therefore they make a conscious decision *not* to identify as Wiccan, just as you wouldn't say you go to a school you don't actually go to.

As for those Witches who have been practicing their Craft entirely independently of Wicca all along—even if their form has some similarities with what we now call Gardnerian and/or Alexandrian Wicca—well, they don't want to be mistaken for members of a club they never even considered joining, particularly when it seems to them to be a huge misrepresentation of their paths.

For some of these folks, the issue with Wicca is its perceived public popularity, which goes quite against the secretive (or at least low-profile-keeping) nature of the Witchcraft they're familiar with.

For others, the widespread acceptance of Eclecticism—the "do what makes sense for you" ethos of much of modern Witchcraft—is seen as a distinctly Wiccan trend that discounts their personal sense of long-standing tradition.

Whatever the reason, it's clear that there are many Witches who do not want to be mistaken for Wiccans.

There are plenty of Wiccans, for that matter, who don't want their particular practice of the Craft confused with other, non-Wiccan forms. (Some Wiccans, particularly those who don't practice magic, don't want to be called "Witches" either.)

So in the spirit of keeping the peace, and in order to get a better sense of what constitutes "Traditional" Witchcraft in these contemporary times, let's take a look at some key aspects of Wicca that can help define the differences, while keeping in mind that Wicca has its own.

WICCA AND DEITY

One of the most obvious elements that distinguishes Wicca from just about all other forms of Witchcraft is the belief in and worship of a pair of supreme deities—the Goddess and the God. These are the two deities honored at the Wiccan altar.

While covens and individuals may worship individual, "patron" gods and goddesses from one or more older pagan system—such as Dionysus and Diana from the Greek pantheon or Cernunnos and Brigid from the Celtic tradition—these "lesser" deities are seen as "aspects" of the all-encompassing Goddess and God.

According to the Wiccan belief system, this pair is responsible for all creation in the Universe, and each plays different roles in the cycles of life during the course of the year.

For example, the Goddess is both the mother of the God, metaphorically giving birth to him at the Winter Solstice, and his mate, coupling with him at Beltane to ensure the continuation of the life cycle. The God is represented by the sun, and the moon represents the Goddess.

Much of Wiccan ritual practice is focused on these deities. They also figure into magical correspondences, with particular colors, herbs, stones, etc. attributed to them.

More traditional Wiccans will refer to the Horned God, rather than simply "the God."

The Horned God is essentially a synthesis of male deities found across many older European traditions, and is associated with virility and prowess in the hunt—the acquisition of food, which is essential to life.

And a closer look at the Goddess reveals a "triple" quality—as the Goddess is associated with the Moon, she has three different phases, or incarnations. The first is the maiden, represented by the waxing phase after the New Moon. The mother aspect is associated with the Full Moon, followed by the crone, or waning Moon which leads to the "dark of the Moon" just before the next New Moon, when the cycle starts again.

These phases are seen to have differing functions in terms of magic. For example, a Wiccan Witch will appeal to the Maiden aspect of the Goddess when calling in a new love relationship.

Indeed, the Goddess turns out to be a rather more complex concept than the God, most likely given the association with the role of the female in human reproduction (which is obviously far more involved than the male's).

It's not uncommon to find the Goddess getting more attention in ritual and magic among some Eclectic Wiccans (who do tend to be female more often than male). However, the emphasis on the Goddess may also be a result of the male domination of deity in Western religions (not to mention in societies in general).

Newcomers to Wicca often find the focus on the female to be an invigorating change of pace. In fact, there's a significant branch of Wicca—usually called "Dianic" Wicca, after the Greek goddess—that essentially ignores the God altogether.

Traditional Witchcraft, by contrast, doesn't recognize any deities as being "supreme" or superior over human beings.

Non-Wiccan Witches may believe in a Goddess and God—and some Traditional paths do work with a Horned God—but they see deities as being inherent in nature, not residing on some higher plane of existence that can't be accessed by human beings.

There is no hierarchy involved in either the cosmology or the actual practice of Witchcraft. Deities may be acknowledged and honored, but they are not "worshipped." They are not appealed to for assistance in magical workings, but rather worked with in partnership.

There's also no common framework for relating to deity in non-Wiccan Witchcraft.

As mentioned above, some do recognize and work with a sort of "all-purpose" pair of deities called the Goddess and the God. Others, like Wiccans, may have personal affinities with specific deities from any number of older pantheons, though most would stick to gods or goddesses of European origin, rather than "borrowing" from Egypt or another more remote region.

Still others will only work with local deities with traditions in their region. A Traditional Witch living in Wales, for example, might have a spiritual connection to the god Arawn, but wouldn't see the point in trying to work with Toth from the Egyptian pantheon.

When it comes to the Triple Goddess, most Traditional Witches will tell you that that's strictly a Wiccan thing—although, as noted earlier, this was likely Robert Cochrane's somewhat unintentional contribution to Wicca.

Those who don't follow Cochrane's Craft or any of its offshoots are not likely to recognize a Triple Goddess, especially those who take a more reconstructionist or otherwise "Traditional" approach to their practice.

Historically, there are some examples of goddesses with triple functions—such as the Celtic Brigh, goddess of healing, poetry, and smithcraft—but they aren't associated with the roles of mother, maiden, and crone, or with phases of the Moon.

Evidence of ancient worship of a virgin/mother/hag deity has been found outside of Europe, but Traditional Witches tend to stick to their own geographical heritage, and see the Triple Goddess as a specifically Wiccan adaptation of "the old religion."

Other non-Wiccan Witches don't relate to the concept of "deity" at all.

They may communicate with what they perceive as spirits of the land, and/or their own personal ancestral guides, all of which are on equal footing with the Witch, rather than "above" her.

Still others might resonate more with the concept that everything in the entire Universe is all one, and speak with "Spirit" as a whole, rather than individual aspects—be they deities, spirits, or other types of entities—of that whole.

Indeed, the ways in which "deity" plays out (or doesn't) in Witchcraft is incredibly varied, and with the exception of those who follow specific forms or schools of Witchcraft, is very much up to the individual Witch.

WICCA AND REINCARNATION

A few other elements of the Wiccan belief system are worth noting here, as they tend to be viewed as distinctly Wiccan.

Perhaps the most significant one is the belief in reincarnation.

Wicca assumes reincarnation as part of the larger life cycle. Each of us is here to learn particular lessons about life in human form before moving on to the next life, or lesson, until our souls reach the point where we no longer feel the need to come to "school" on Earth.

This view of life brings with it the concept of karma—the idea that every action we take has a reaction, which factors into our life circumstances due to actions we took in past lives, and actions we take within this life, including magical action.

This phenomenon forms the basis for the Wiccan moral code of "harm to none" and the "Threefold Law," which we'll take a closer look at below.

Non-Wiccan Witches may or may not subscribe to these beliefs.

Traditional Witches tend to view the concepts of reincarnation and karma as being Eastern mystical influences, and therefore not part of the tradition of Witchcraft. (Their views of the afterlife vary, but often include the notion that departed souls return as spirits of the land, rather than as reincarnated people.)

However, these Eastern concepts did influence many Western spiritual thinkers of the occult revival that gave rise to modern Witchcraft, and so it's certainly possible to be a Witch who believes in reincarnation but does not identify with Wicca.

WICCA AND CORRESPONDENCES

Another difference between Wiccans and other Witches is the emphasis on magical correspondences.

This is an elaborate system of associations linking both tangible things (like crystals and herbs) and intangible concepts (like days of the week and directions) to specific magical properties.

The associations can be based on astrology, cosmology, numerology, the classical elements, and other belief systems that provide Wiccans with specific pathways to follow when pursuing magical aims.

For example, Friday is thought to be best for working love spells, as it associated with Venus, the planet of love. Rose quartz and red candles also have love associations, so a spell involving both of these, worked on a Friday, would be considered likely to have extra success.

Most Wiccan spellwork is performed with correspondences in mind, and many Wiccans will only work particular spells if and when they have the exact right ingredients according to correspondences.

While non-Wiccans generally recognize that correspondences can be useful, they are not overly concerned with taking advantage of them, focusing instead on the inner focus and strength of personal energy needed to work successful magic.

WICCA AND "THE WHEEL OF THE YEAR"

It can be argued that observing the changing of the seasons and the cycles of nature is an inherent part of all Witchcraft, but Wicca has its own particular "take" on this concept that forms the heart of its practice: the eight "Sabbats" and 13 "Esbats" (or Full Moon celebrations) that form the Wheel of the Year.

The Sabbats are considered the solar holidays and consist of both solstices, both equinoxes, and 4 "cross-quarter days" which are based on European pagan festivals of earlier centuries.

The Wheel has a specific mythological story of death and rebirth, featuring the Goddess and the God as the symbolic characters, as mentioned above.

Each Sabbat is kind of like a "chapter" in the continually revolving story, and each chapter creates a specific theme for the ritual that brings Wiccans together to celebrate.

These themes follow the typical agricultural growing cycle of the Northern Hemisphere, with late summer and autumn rituals related to harvest, and early spring and summer Sabbats focused on fertility and abundance.

Non-Wiccan Witches may or may not pay attention to the solstices, equinoxes, and/or cross-quarter dates. Those who do are very unlikely to engage in any elaborate rituals.

They may celebrate with a special meal or light a designated candle, but the attention is on the seasonal implications of the holiday, rather than on a metaphorical story about deities. They may or may not recognize these points along the solar calendar as "Sabbats," or refer to any activity on the Full Moon as an "Esbat."

Furthermore, a Traditional Witch may choose to honor the festival of Beltane in May, but completely ignore Lughnassa (also known as Lammas) in early August.

By contrast, celebrating the points along the Wheel of the Year is treated almost as a requirement for Wiccans, and this tends to be the main reason that covens exist. It gives this relatively new religion a means of structure and focus that isn't found (or particularly desired) in Traditional Witchcraft.

WICCA AND RITUAL

Perhaps the biggest and most significant difference between Wicca and other Witchcraft is Wicca's emphasis on formal ritual.

This is not to say that other forms of Witchcraft *don't* observe rituals, but that in Wicca, ritual is at the center of the practice, and is generally rather elaborate and ceremonial.

This can be traced back to Gerald Gardner and his original Bricket Wood coven. As he put together the ritual material for his coveners to follow, Gardner drew on influences from many sources that involved ceremonial or "high magic," such as could be found in the rituals of the Freemasons as well as the Hermetic Order of the Golden Dawn, which had taken root in the English occult revival of the late 19th century and was still influential during Gardner's time.

Gardner's initial material was reworked and added to by other members of the original movement that came to be called "Wicca," and as this material has been handed down from covener to covener over the decades, it has been altered and adapted by different groups, but the core elements have generally been kept by anyone identifying as a practicing Wiccan.

One primary component of Wiccan ritual that isn't seen in other forms of Witchcraft is the casting of the circle.

At the start of each ritual, Wiccans "cast" a circle around the area where the ritual will take place. They may actually mark out the circle with sea salt, herbs, or other magical items, or they may "draw" it invisibly with a wand, finger, or other tool.

The circle creates a border between the mundane, ordinary world and the sacred space where the ritual and/or spellwork happens. It serves to focus the magical energy in one place, where it can be directed according to the practitioner's will.

At the end of the ritual, the circle is "taken down" and any lingering magical energy is "grounded," often by storing it in a ritual tool.

The act of casting a circle, which can be done subtlety and without attracting unwanted attention by a seasoned practitioner, can provide a convenient means of exiting the plane of ordinary reality and entering into a space where communion with the divine and/or magic can be performed, anywhere at anytime.

Another ritual component found only in Wicca is the calling of the "quarters" (or "Watchtowers" in some traditions).

The quarters are related both to the four cardinal directions (North, East, South, and West) and the four classical elements (Earth, Air, Fire, and Water).

There are many different variations of this aspect of ritual, which may have one or more purpose: to honor the forces of nature through the elements and directions, to invoke protection from these forces, and/or to summon assistance in magical workings from them.

Many Wiccans believe in and work with what are called "elementals": unseen spirits of earth, air, fire, and water, each with their own characteristics or "personalities." Others simply acknowledge and honor the inherent powers of the elements and their contributions to the physical reality of life on Earth.

Whatever form this step takes, it's usually performed shortly after casting the circle, and before the main ritual work is begun. Likewise, at the end of ritual, the quarters will be thanked and "released" before the circle is taken down.

While both of these steps will most likely be followed in any kind of Wiccan ritual worship, such as a Sabbat or Esbat celebration, not all Wiccans will perform them every single time they undertake magical work. This depends on the individual's tradition (or lack thereof) and level of comfort with working outside the framework of established Wiccan ritual.

Non-Wiccans, however, are unlikely to ever "summon" elemental spirits or directional energies by calling the quarters. While they might request the aid of particular land spirits, or even the energies of one or more elements suited to the purpose of their particular magical work, Traditional Witches view the calling of the quarters as being unnecessarily manipulative or controlling, and would not want to work with energies or spirits that had not arrived of their own free will.

As for casting the sacred circle, Traditional Witches and other non-Wiccans consider it unnecessary, since *all* space, everywhere on Earth, is seen as being inherently sacred.

Finally, the emphasis and reliance on specific magical tools in ritual and spellwork is a fairly uniquely Wiccan development.

There's a rather long list of altar tools considered to be essential to Wiccan ritual, though some are more "mandatory" than others. The cup, wand, athame, and pentacle are borrowed from ceremonial magic, while the cauldron and broom come from older associations. (Incense and candles, of course, are found in many diverse spiritual traditions, including some sects of Christianity.)

This isn't to say that non-Wiccan Witches don't use any tools—there may even be some overlap here with Traditionals and others, but only Wiccans seem to view them as necessary.

For the Traditional Witch, the only necessary "tools" are the mind and its focused intent. Just as correspondences can be useful but aren't necessary, so it is with tools of ritual and spellwork.

At this point, the comparison between Wicca and other forms of Witchcraft can make Wicca seem to take a very method-driven, almost mechanical approach to mysticism and magic.

While it's true that non-Wiccan Witches are unlikely to feel the need to employ the elements of ritual described above, for Wiccans they are clearly worth practicing.

Particularly for a busy Witch living in the modern urban world, "devices" such as the circle and the use of ritual tools can make it easier to shake off a hard day at work and tune in more quickly to divine presence, whether for a mid-week Sabbat celebration, a New Moon working, or simply an "ordinary" spell.

This approach can also be useful for those new to Witchcraft who may or may not ultimately choose the Wiccan path, but can certainly learn something from it along the way.

OTHER SPECIFICALLY WICCAN PRACTICES

A few other key differences deserve a mention here, specifically regarding ritual dress code, initiation, and coven leadership.

You may or may not be familiar with the term "skyclad," which is how Wiccans refer to their practice of performing rituals in the nude.

Gerald Gardner was a nudist before he founded what became Wicca, and so he incorporated this preference into his coven's practice. Since then, some Wiccans have chosen to continue this tradition, but it is by no means a requirement—unless you're joining a coven that specifically works skyclad.

Other Wiccans wear special ritual robes, usually (but not always) black in color, both in solo practice and as coven members.

Still others wear no special clothing at all. They may wear special jewelry, such as a pentacle on a chain or a treasured crystal or mineral stone, but otherwise practice in street clothes.

Traditional, non-Wiccan Witchcraft, on the other hand, doesn't tend to involve any sort of dress code.

As their traditions come from the days when it would have been very dangerous to be thought to be practicing magic or having non-Christian religious leanings, these practitioners definitely don't see a benefit in being identifiable as Witches. Furthermore, ritual clothing, like ritual tools, just isn't seen as a necessity in their brand of spirituality.

That being said, there are some non-Wiccan traditions that incorporate some kind of body adornment, particularly for coven rituals. "Skyclad," however, remains a Wiccan institution.

While both Wicca and non-Wiccan Witchcraft usually involve a tradition of initiation of some sort, the philosophy and practice of initiation can differ widely.

Traditionally, Wiccan initiation into a coven is a highly ritualized ceremony in which initiates are both blindfolded and naked, showing their trust in both the Goddess and God as well as the coven members. Often, someone seeking to join Wicca in this way will have to study the beliefs and practices for a year and a day before being eligible for initiation.

There is also a series of "degrees" in many branches of Wicca that can be pursued if one wishes to do so—somewhat like attending graduate school after college. The first degree is obtained upon the initial initiation; upon further study and practice, one can move on to the second degree, and then the third. The specific requirements for each degree will depend on the particular tradition one is following.

As the spread of Wicca over the second half of the 20th century gave rise to the solitary and/or Eclectic practitioner, new Wiccans who either couldn't find a coven or didn't wish to join one began to self-initiate, either according to suggested rituals (such as those offered by Wiccan authors Raymond Buckland and, later, Scott Cunningham) or making up their own. In the 21st century, it's likely that far more contemporary Wiccans are self-initiating into their own Eclectic practices than are following a traditional route.

Traditional Witchcraft approaches initiation differently, though it's difficult to go into much detail here, due to the fact that so much of the practice of many Traditionals is kept secret.

While it's certain that initiates do have to prepare themselves through study, just as they do in Wicca, it's safe to say that there's not a lot of blindfolded nudity involved in a Traditional initiation (though it's certainly a possibility in some cases).

At any rate, what is termed "initiation" in non-Wiccan forms of the Craft can only be conferred on a newcomer by someone else who has been initiated into the lineage—in other words, there is no true "self-initiation" into Traditional Witchcraft.

However, because so many traditions within Traditional Witchcraft remain secretive and never actively seek new members, it's far less common for someone interested in these forms of the Craft to find a coven or other group to join. Therefore, a lot of contemporary non-Wiccan Witches study and practice as solitaries, and will perform a self-*dedication* ritual, if and when they see fit to do so.

The main distinction here is that initiated Traditional Witches are seen as having license to pass on their traditions, whereas solitary "dedicated" Witches do not.

The most fundamental difference, however, is in how Traditional Witches view the end goal of initiation—in other words, what, exactly, the initiate is dedicating herself or himself *to*.

While Wiccan initiation is focused on the newcomer's dedication to studying and advancing along the path of Wicca, non-Wiccans view the dedication as being to the service of "the gods," or, as some would put it, "Nature." In other words, the emphasis is on the relationship between the initiate and the divine, as opposed to the initiate and the "path" itself.

Related to initiation is the tradition of *hierarchy* in Wicca. The distinctions between degrees creates a potential for hierarchy within any given coven, as seen in the terms "High Priestess" and "High Priest."

While the degree system is meant to provide opportunities for deepening one's practice of Wicca, it does, unfortunately, appeal to some people's sense of ego, and you'll find some amount of "holier than thou" attitude about this among some Wiccan authors, particularly on the Internet.

Folks who let their "degrees" and titles go to their heads are definitely in the minority, but they can be among the loudest voices out there. So if you're reading around and encounter any writers who claim to be supreme authorities on Wicca—particularly if they're egotistical about it—feel free to ignore them and move on.

The titles "High Priestess" and "High Priest" were most likely inspired by ceremonial magic, where hierarchy is a fundamental part of the system of learning.

In most of the non-Wiccan world of Witchcraft, there are no "degrees" of study and there is no hierarchy.

Coven leaders will be referred to as Priestess or Priest, but only to signify that they're the leaders of the coven—they have no status above any other member.

Everyone is equal, no matter where they are in their personal study along a given path.

THE WICCAN MORAL CODE

Finally, Wicca differs from other forms of Witchcraft in its philosophy of appropriate and inappropriate uses of magic.

One of the first things aspiring Wiccans learn about the practice of magic is the phrase "an it harm none, do what ye will." This is a somewhat artificially antiquated way of saying "as long as it harms no one, and it's what you want, go ahead."

The phrase comes from a longer piece of verse in couplets called "The Wiccan Rede," which contains other instructions, advice, and ideas regarding the proper practice of Wicca. However, this phrase all by itself is often referred to as "The "Wiccan Rede."

The basic idea is that Wiccans should only practice magic that will not cause any harm to anyone, whether the harm is intentional or unintentional. This obviously rules out curses, hexes, etc. but also applies to any magic that could be manipulative or interfere with another person's free will. (Love spells are a classic example of magic that may seem to be harmless, but are actually inconsiderate of the object of desire's personal wishes and path.)

In fact, many Wiccan spells will end with a phrase like "for the good of all and harm to none" to ensure that no unintentional negative effects result from the manifestation of the spell.

A related belief is the Threefold Law, which holds that any magic performed by a Witch will come back to her/him three times, and serves as an extra incentive to be sure of one's means and motives when working a spell.

Witchcraft traditionally doesn't make a distinction between helpful and harmful magic, seeing magical energy as inherently neutral. And, outside of Wicca, there really isn't a "moral code."

Rather than the Threefold Law, many non-Wiccan Witches believe in the "Return of Energy," or the "Law of Cause and Effect," which states that for every action, there is an equal and opposite reaction.

Knowing this, non-Wiccan Witches take responsibility for their actions rather than emphasizing a morally-based "positive magic only" set of rules.

They might cast a curse or a hex out of self-protection, and see no ethical problem with doing so. There are some Witches who would go even further and say that negative magic has its place if it serves the aim of the practitioner, self-defense or not.

Indeed, the question of ethics in the world of non-Wiccan Witchcraft can have quite a variety of answers, which we will revisit later in this guide.

RESPECTING THE DIFFERENCES

As mentioned above, if you're reading around on the Internet about Witchcraft, you may discover no small bit of rancor among those who don't want to be associated with Wicca on any level. There's also plenty of outright Wicca-bashing out there of late, most likely due to its rapidly increasing popularity among people who might be described as more "mainstream" than those who were drawn to the Craft in prior decades.

Those who value the tradition of secrecy may be among the most irked by Wicca's spread, as many Wiccans will go so far as to share their spells and rituals online for all the world to see.

Others with attachments to ideas of spiritual and familial lineage and age-old tradition simply can't bring themselves to take Wicca and its relatively very new origins seriously.

However, there's plenty of room in the Universe for diverse approaches to Witchcraft and to spirituality in general. Whatever the differences, and whatever the circumstances of Wicca's origins, it is an authentic branch of Witchcraft with earnest and, on the whole, well-meaning followers.

Furthermore, as some writers on the topic have noted, the rise and spread of Wicca has actually helped to make Witchcraft more acceptable to a much wider segment of the mainstream population than ever before in history.

Whether or not an individual Witch wants her or his belief system "out there for the world to see," all Witches can appreciate that their chosen form of spirituality is less likely than ever before to make them targets for trouble.

For that, all Witches (and even those practitioners of the Craft who don't call themselves Witches) may actually owe Wicca a debt of gratitude.

CONTEMPORARY WITCHCRAFT: WITCHDOM FOR THE 21ST CENTURY

The word "contemporary," as we're using it here, means "belonging to or occurring in the present."

Strictly speaking, this means that every form of Witchcraft described in Part Two of this guide is contemporary Witchcraft. Whether it takes the form of old folk magic, British Traditional, Gardnerian Wicca, or Sabbatic Craft, as long as it's being practiced by at least one living person at this time, it's contemporary Witchcraft.

(Some would argue that Sabbatic Craft and other forms still being developed at this moment are really just contemporary and not traditional, given that they're much younger than, say, the Feri Tradition. It's a fair point, but this guide will respect the terms and identifiers that practitioners choose for themselves.)

However, for our purposes, the focus here will be on a few distinctly contemporary paths of the Craft, including Hedgewitchery, Green Witchery, and Kitchen Witchery, as well as that great catch-all term, Eclectic Witchcraft.

WHAT IS AN ECLECTIC WITCH?

The largest sector of contemporary Witchcraft is probably Eclectic Witchcraft, which is a catch-all term for Witches who don't follow a particular form, path, or tradition of the Craft, but rather freely choose from various influences to build their practice, and often create, or intuit, much of it themselves.

Many, many Wiccans fall into this category, which seemed to spread almost as quickly in the United States as Traditional Wicca itself—perhaps even more quickly.

This was in part because of the rise in available information about Wicca, but it was also because interested would-be Wiccans were unable to find a coven to join in their area. People began to decide that since they couldn't access a path of initiatory lineage, then initiation through another Witch didn't really have to be mandatory, and the solitary Witch was born (or "reborn," depending on your perspective on the history of the Old Religion).

Once solitary practice was an option, the freedom to keep departing from tradition and inventing new practices knew no limits (a quintessential American quality), giving rise to the Eclectic Witch.

It was this fairly rebellious characteristic of modern American Witchcraft that really created the gulf between the "Traditional Craft" of Britain and what was now called Wicca in the New World.

Again, it can be pointed out that this is more or less how every established and recognized form of the Craft since the turn of the twentieth century was initially started—by synthesizing material from older traditions to create new paths—but the difference here is that Eclectics aren't necessarily interested in signing others on to the way they practice.

Eclectic Witches tend to be solitary, or may be associated with a circle or group that they share ideas with, but they're less likely to join a coven, much less start one. (Eclectic covens do exist, but since the nature of a coven is to have everyone doing something in the same way, it's not quite the "create-your-own-path" experience that it is for Eclectic solitaries.)

An Eclectic Witch may incorporate some Wiccan beliefs and practices but still not identify as a Wiccan. Similarly, an Eclectic may incorporate some reconstructionist Witchcraft without adopting the "recon" moniker.

The big draw of Eclecticism, in fact, may be just how easy it is to avoid the snare of contested terminology that this guide has been detailing throughout Part Two. Even if your practice is rooted in a particular tradition, such as Wicca, Feri, or Sabbatic Craft, but you don't follow it to the letter, you can put "Eclectic" in front of it for an accurate representation of your path.

Indeed Eclectic Witchcraft can be thought of as the "melting pot" of Witchcraft, where various traditions come together and form new combinations at every turn.

OTHER AVENUES OF CONTEMPORARY WITCHCRAFT

As mentioned earlier, there's just no way to identify every single new form of the Craft being practiced today.

That being said, a few other terms have emerged fairly recently that describe some common paths of interest: Hedgewitchery, Green Witchery, and Kitchen Witchery.

(These terms show up in both Wiccan and non-Wiccan contexts, so that you may come across "Green Wicca" or "Kitchen Wicca," which may differ substantially from their non-Wiccan counterparts, but are still coming from the same basic source.)

Although some practitioners of one or more of these forms would call them traditions in their own right, they can also be thought of more as *approaches* to Witchcraft that comprise just one part of an individual Witch's overall practice.

For example, someone who practices Kitchen Witchery may not do any other form of Witchcraft—no magic, no belief in deity, etc.—or she may use her Kitchen Witchery skills in addition to other forms of the Craft.

While the terms for these paths may have come into popularity fairly recently, each form is rooted in traditional Witchcraft practices, often going back several centuries or more. In fact, many of the practices involved in these approaches are arguably as old as humanity itself.

HEDGEWITCHERY

Hedgewitchery is among the most shamanic forms of Witchcraft, focusing on the interaction between the Witch and the spirit world (or "otherworld," as it is often called).

The word "shaman" originally comes from ancient religions of North Asia, but, like "witchcraft," it has been used by anthropologists in recent decades in a global sense.

Shamans are individuals who engage in altered states of consciousness, or trancework, used for communication with ancestors and spirits, usually for the purposes of divination and/or healing. It can be argued that all pre-industrial cultures have shamans and shamanic practices, and they are found extensively in many Native American cultures, as well as Africa, Oceania, and other parts of the world.

Hedgewitches, in their practice, may draw on the "shamanic" traditions found in European Witchcraft, such as those found among the cunning folk of England or in similar traditions in Italy, Hungary, and Scandinavia.

They may also branch out and borrow practices from other cultures, including Native American traditions, though doing so can be controversial, as such actions may be seen as a form of cultural appropriation.

The word "hedgewitch" (alternatively called "hedgecraft") is derived from a Saxon/Old English word *haegtessa*, which means "hedge rider."

In pre-industrial rural areas of Europe, villages and towns were often bordered by hedgerows, keeping wild animals out and marking the boundary between civilization and wilderness. Walking beyond these hedges meant you were taking your chances in the wild.

The "hedge" involved in Hedgewitchery is not a fence made of shrubs, but a metaphor for the boundary between the mundane world and the spirit world. "Riding the hedge" is another way of saying "walking between the worlds," which is the essential way in which these types of Witches accomplish their work.

A Hedgewitch will access the spirit world through various means, including drumming, chanting, ecstatic dance, visualization, meditation, and/or the use of entheogens, or hallucinogenic plants. (This last method is not recommended unless you are under the supervision of a *very* experienced practitioner, and even then should be approached with extreme caution!)

Once there, the Hedgewitch might glean useful information about healing herbs, a significant event in the future, or other types of knowledge. Over time, these experiences enhance and strengthen the Witch's overall practice of the Craft.

GREEN WITCHERY

As you might suspect from the name, Green Witches are very much involved with the environment and its countless blessings.

The central focus of Green Witchery is on working with the magical energetic properties of everything that grows in the ground—trees, herbs, flowers, and other plants. These energies can be used in healing, divination, and other magic.

Green Witches may work with certain plants by using folklore that dates back hundreds of years, right alongside modern research into their medicinal properties. They understand the multiple properties of the ingredients they work with on both the mundane and spiritual levels.

For example, chamomile is known to have physically calming effects on the body, and is used to relieve various kinds of tension and inflammation. And one of its magical properties is the ability to release feelings of anger or emotional pain. A Green Witch will be aware of both of these aspects of chamomile's energy when deciding whether to use it for a particular situation, such as for someone suffering from headaches related to heartbreak or frustration in love.

Green Witches tend to be gardeners, foragers, or both, and are likely to be skilled in making potions, tinctures, teas, oils, and other remedies for physical, emotional, and magical needs. They may stick mostly to crafting the above-mentioned remedies for physical use, or they may have more of a focus on spells and charms. The type of path that a Green Witch follows is always individual to the practitioner.

Green Witches may also have a little (or a lot) of the "Hedge Witch" in them, choosing the most effective herbs to use for a particular purpose by listening for instructions from the spirit world, and/or from the plants themselves.

However, it's important to note here that the most successful Green Witchery involves extensive study in herbalism, and that *no one, Witch or otherwise, should under any circumstances use an herb they are unfamiliar with for any purpose*. Plenty of plants are toxic and even deadly when consumed by humans, while others—such as poison oak or poison ivy—cause problems just when touched!

If you're a budding Witch with an affinity for plants—even if you have already developed an excellent sixth-sense relationship with nature—always research everything you plan to work with. Hunches and inklings are great, but they're no substitute for tried-and-true knowledge.

In fact, looking up your potential herb of choice will actually help you strengthen your intuitive relationship with nature, as you'll be able to get confirmation that your hunch was on target!

KITCHEN WITCHERY

The Kitchen Witch is found, of course, in the kitchen, and it can be argued that this is where the transformative powers of magic are most obvious—even though we generally take this kind of transformation for granted.

Centuries ago, before electricity made the process of cooking food so much easier, the fire—or hearth—was where raw ingredients were transformed into nourishing, delicious meals.

Given that so much more effort went into the production of food back then—not just in the cooking but in the growing, hunting, and preparation of ingredients—the sacred nature of the Earth's bounty and blessings was much more actively recognized.

Rituals and blessings accompanied every aspect of food production, from appealing to the gods for a successful hunt, to blessing the crops brought in from the harvest, and giving sacrifices of food to the spirits as thanks for the bounty.

The Kitchen Witch retains this attitude of reverence for food and its many magical, nourishing properties.

These Witches consider every aspect of cooking to be part of a magical process, and put magic into their homemade creations, whether it be a hearty stew, a rustic loaf of bread, or a delicious dessert.

They may charge their herbs and other ingredients with specific magical intention before use, say a chant or a blessing over the food as it's being prepared, and/or light candles at the dining table as part of a silent spell for peace and love before calling the family to dinner.

In short, Kitchen Witches infuse every aspect of meal preparation with magic. Looked at in this light, it's no wonder that the cauldron has remained such a steadfast symbol of magic and transformation in the Witching world!

Of course, Kitchen Witchery is not limited to culinary work— medicinal concoctions such as teas, tinctures, and ointments may be part of the Kitchen Witch's repertoire, as well as charms and potions, and even homemade candles.

As with Green Witchery, the Kitchen Witch may not practice any kind of formal or ceremonial magic, keeping the focus instead on the tangible world of the kitchen and all of the skills that successful Kitchen Witchery requires.

NATURAL COMPLEMENTS

Again, these three paths just listed are not hard-and-fast categories and are by no means mutually exclusive. An individual Witch may actually practice all three of these forms, particularly since they naturally complement each other.

Learning and progress in one of these areas is very conducive to growth in another as an automatic "side effect."

For example, the more one gets to know and experience the plant world, the more likely the spirits of the plants themselves will begin to communicate with the practitioner. And experimenting in the kitchen with one or more herbs is one of the best ways to compliment one's trancework, bringing the knowledge from the spirit world into practical use in the mundane world!

As mentioned above, all three of these forms can be paths woven into larger Traditional or Eclectic practices, or simply practiced in their own right. And while all three are rooted in very old ways of living, they are certainly enhanced by the knowledge available to us here in the Information Age.

THE MANY
WAYS OF THE WITCH

By now, you should have a solid understanding of the rich diversity of beliefs and practices that fall under the umbrella term of "Witchcraft."

Whether you resonate more with those paths that can be accurately labeled "Traditional," or with more modern forms, including specific Wiccan systems and/or Eclectic approaches, you have hopefully gained a sense of the wonderful variety of options available to the contemporary practitioner.

Of course, some paths are more open to newcomers than others, and respect for those who don't wish to share their closely-guarded practices with the outside world is important.

After all, if a particular path isn't accessible to you, then it's safe to say that it isn't meant for you. In fact, if you're serious about pursuing Witchcraft, it's equally safe to say that the path you're meant for will meet you halfway.

In Part Three, we'll examine some of the common beliefs and practices at the heart of much of contemporary Witchcraft.

These include views of the natural world and the spirit world, and how they interact with the human-made world that we often refer to as "civilization."

We'll also take a look at a few frameworks for understanding how and why magic works, as well as common purposes of magical practice.

Of course, this overview will consist of generalizations that don't apply to every practitioner, but will provide a clearer sense of how

Witches experience and co-create with the forces at work in the delightfully mysterious Universe.

PART THREE

SPIRITUALITY AND MAGIC IN CONTEMPORARY WITCHCRAFT

OBSERVANCE
AND PRACTICE

If you're just starting out in your reading about Witchcraft, you may have plenty of questions of what it is that Witches actually *do*.

And if you've read this far into this guide, you know that there are more answers to this question than there's room for in one single book—in fact, there are an infinite number of answers, since each Witch's practice is unique.

This is especially true of Eclectic Witches and others who practice solitary forms, but it's also true of Traditional Witches, who are always interpreting the Craft they've inherited from the past in new ways that are relevant in their own lives. Even the most orthodox Wiccan covens will adjust and adapt practices to a certain extent, provided they stay within the boundaries of their particular tradition.

This is because, of course, Witchcraft is not a "religion' in the conventional, monotheistic sense that we've come to understand the word. There is no scripture, no holy text, no set of written instructions that applies to every practitioner. There is no authority and no uniformly agreed-upon set of principles. This non-standardization is often a significant part of the appeal of Witchcraft to newcomers.

There is, however, a great number of beliefs and practices that Witches have in common. For example, it would not be unusual for most Witches to:

- Greet the sunrise with a thought or prayer of gratitude and a conscious setting of intentions for the day ahead.

- Clean and lay out crystals and other gemstones to charge in the sunlight.

- Brew a tea from loose dried herbs as a remedy for a physical or emotional need.
- Engage in a daily meditation or visualization practice.
- Leave offerings to the spirit of a particular beloved tree, creek, or boulder.
- Light a candle at the full moon to celebrate abundance and set an intention to attract even more.
- Seek advice about a situation from Tarot cards, a scrying bowl, or other form of divination.
- Maintain an altar to, and a regular practice of communing with, a deity.
- make and bless a charm satchel to carry to a job interview.
- Take a ritual bath to release old attachments to a person, place, or event from the past.

Some of these actions may seem more unusual or esoteric than others. Making tea, for example, is a fairly mundane activity that millions of non-Witches perform every day. (The difference, of course, is that Witches will very intentionally direct magical energy into the process of making, and then drinking, the tea, whereas most mainstream people in Western society will simply boil the kettle, pour the water, and sip without giving any of it much thought.)

On the other hand, leaving a pinch of dried herbs or a few drops of milk or honey at the base of a hundred-year-old oak tree might seem rather out of the ordinary, as might seeing images in a bowl of still water. To a Witch, however, each of these activities is equally normal, and each contributes to a magical and interesting daily life that is both full of mystery and grounded in reality at the same time.

The two main currents running through the life of a Witch may be thought of as *observance* (or "spirituality,") and *practice*, (or "magic").

Observance refers to the contemplative and devotional activities of a Witch, and might include the celebrating of solar holidays (the Equinoxes and Solstices), old pagan festival days such as Imbolc and Beltane, and Full Moons and New Moons, in addition to the above-mentioned revering of objects in nature.

Of course, not all Witches incorporate these elements in their practice, and many will reject even the term "spiritual" to describe themselves. The Craft is an art as much as anything else, and some practitioners see it only as an art, not a religion.

Nonetheless, it's safe to say that the majority of Witchcraft practiced today has a spiritual component of some kind, even if it simply takes the form of consciously interacting with the unseen forces that help to shape our daily lives.

As for magic, it's also true that not everyone under the umbrella term of "Witchcraft" practices this ancient art, but those who leave it out are also in the minority, and tend to be found particularly in the Wiccan community. The rest of the Witching world does practice magic, and this is where the word "practice" becomes particularly relevant.

Magic, like medicine or law, is a *practice*. It is a set of skills that one develops over time, through rigorous study, trial and error, and the gradual accumulation of experience.

In other words, magic takes a lot of practice!

While some aspiring Witches may experience success in their spellwork surprisingly quickly, it's not at all unusual to fail a few times before one begins to get the hang of the mentality and focus required to see results.

Part of the struggle for beginners is often a sense of skepticism that, despite effort, has been ingrained in us through our culture of science and "rationalism" for the past couple of centuries.

It can be hard, no matter how much one wants to, to let go of old beliefs about the way the world works. We like proof, and when beginning Witches don't get it right away after working a spell, it can cause their doubt and resistance to belief to grow even stronger.

And it doesn't help that the word "magic" really has been associated with pure fantasy since long before any of us was born. If you don't come from a Witching family, and if you don't have friends with the same inclinations as you, it can be a lonely and uphill road to truly understanding that magic is real, that it works, and that it's going on all around us, undetected, more than we realize.

For the benefit of the skeptics, we'll examine a few ways in which the phenomenon of magic has been explained over the centuries, as well as some modern parallels to these theories found in recent scientific discoveries.

But first, we'll take a look at a few basic underlying beliefs that tend to inform most Witches' work, interweaving observance with practice in interesting and beautiful ways.

COMMON BELIEFS
IN TRADITIONAL
WITCHCRAFT SYSTEMS

Witchcraft predates our familiar paradigms of scientific inquiry and rationalism, etc., and so it is founded upon much older beliefs, which exist in one form or another around the globe.

As always, these beliefs may be understood and explained differently, depending on the Witch, or Witchcraft tradition, in question, but we can identify a few here that are commonly found in the practices of many who identify as Witches.

ANIMISM

In some ways, it could be argued that animism is the basis, or most fundamental belief, of Witchcraft.

Animism is a worldview that sees absolutely no separation between the material world and the spiritual world.

In contrast to the premise of monotheistic religions like Christianity, where the spirit world (or "Heaven") is a faraway place that the living have no access to during their time on Earth, animism sees the Earth and everything on it as inherently part of the energy of spirit.

Animism is not a religion in and of itself, but a way of being oriented to the world in one's perceptions.

Animistic qualities are at work in many religious belief systems around the world, and are especially found today in African, Native American, and Southeast Asian cultures, among others.

Animism was certainly alive and well in pre-Christian Europe as well, as can be seen in the mythological lore of ancient Germanic and Celtic tribes, and though it has been all but shut out of mainstream rationalist culture, it has held on over the centuries in subtle ways, such as in the presence of "holy wells" throughout Britain and Ireland, which are still visited by Pagans and Christians alike.

There are two "textbook" definitions of animism, and both are applicable to Witchcraft.

The first is the belief that there is a soul, or spirit, in inanimate objects found in nature, such as trees, mountains, rocks, rivers, lakes, etc., as well as in non-human animals.

In some animistic cultures, this "soul" is recognized in some things, but not necessarily others, so that there might be one particular tree in a grove that is considered sacred, while others around it are not.

This doesn't mean that the other trees are considered to be separate from the spirit world, but simply that they don't possess the kind of potent spiritual energy that humans are able to recognize and interact with. The determination of which objects and animals are recognized as having souls would depend on the individual culture or group and their experiences with the land they inhabit.

The second definition of animism is the belief in an unseen force that organizes and powers the material world.

This sense of the word differs from the first in that the focus is not on individual objects, but on the organizing principle of the "big picture"—the idea that everything is interconnected, that all things are imbued with spirit because they were created by spirit. This includes animals and inanimate objects, but can also include non-physical things such as words and metaphors, musical notes, numbers, and other concepts.

This concept of animism is quite similar to pantheism, which is the belief that the *divine* is in all things. The main difference is that pantheism is seen as a religious belief, focusing on the deity or "God" as the unseen force, whereas animism is concerned primarily with the *manifestations*—the objects, animals, words, etc.—that are encountered in the material world.

Whether one's particular belief system and/or experience fits more with the first definition of animism or the second, or both, these concepts are very useful in understanding how Witches relate to the world around them.

Witchcraft certainly involves the belief in, and interaction with, spirits and/or other unseen forces, and more often than not, Witchcraft involves working with physical objects as well as non-physical "things" such as specific visualizations and words used in spells, to achieve magical aims.

And while it is generally said that the power in these objects is the Witch's power moving through them—particularly when it comes to manufactured tools like athames, pentacles, and the like—this doesn't contradict the idea that objects themselves can hold spiritual energy.

As for tools such as herbs, crystals, sea salt, and anything else that comes straight from the Earth, these are generally held to possess their own inherent spiritual energy, which is then combined with or channelled by the Witch for a particular purpose.

NATURE AS SACRED SPACE

If you imagine what the Earth was like for people ten thousand years ago, or even just two thousand, the premise of animism is likely to make more sense than it might today.

Before the development of the scientific method—which does not acknowledge what can't be proven in a fairly narrowly specific manner—and without the noise and distraction of our industrialized modern world, it wouldn't be far-fetched at all to perceive a spiritual presence permeating one's environment.

These days, however, this universal presence can be fairly difficult to pick up on if one is in, say, a shopping mall or an elevator (though it's not impossible). Indeed, those of us living largely urban lives may be more likely to scoff at the animistic perspective than those who live closer to the less-developed parts of the world, where nature's "voice" can still be heard.

Of course, in earlier centuries, nature was a much harsher place to inhabit, particularly in very cold and very hot climates and in places where predatory animals still posed a danger to humans.

Still, nature was the original source of mystery and magic, from the life cycles of the animals to the growth of giant trees from tiny seeds. Even now, with all of our knowledge of biology and botany, etc., it's hard for even the average person not to be awed by an intense thunderstorm or a brilliant sunset.

And while there are some who claim to be "allergic" to any and every aspect of the great outdoors, we often speak of wanting to "get back to nature" as a way of decompressing from our hectic lives, acknowledging with this phrase that we still remember, and long for, our origins.

Witches are no exception, and typically find it easier to commune with the unseen creative force of the Universe—whether they perceive it to be in the form of spirits, deities, or a singular source of divinity—when they are outdoors and surrounded by forest, field, mountains, desert, ocean or canyon.

Those who live in towns and cities will at least make the effort to walk in green spaces and tend gardens—even if the garden is just a few potted plants in a kitchen window—in order to stay connected to the Earth.

Of course, the degree to which nature is part of the work and worldview of any individual Witch could be said to be along a spectrum.

Those practicing Green Witchery may be more apt to work directly with nature in the form of outdoor rituals, a focus on herbal magic, and/or a practice of honoring one or more deities associated with a specific aspect of nature.

Witches who are far less inclined to immerse themselves in the natural world might practice a more highly formalized, ceremonial style of ritual and magic, using more man-made tools like the chalice, athame, and pentacle found in Wicca (although Wicca certainly incorporates a very specifically nature-oriented mythology).

But however one's specific belief system and personal connection with nature shows up in their practice, Witches know that the natural world is where both humans and the Craft began, and it will always be at the root of both.

NON-PHYSICAL ENTITIES

For many Witches, it's not just the physical aspects of nature—rocks, trees, rivers, etc.—that are sacred, but the unseen spirits, deities, and/or other beings who reside there.

Now, as mentioned earlier in this guide, this is a very diverse area of belief in the realm of Witchcraft.

Some Witches may believe in and work with a multitude of non-physical entities, while others may not at all. But a very significant portion of the Witching community would identify some kind of relationship with some kind of unseen guidance or assistance as part of their path in the Craft.

The way in which these entities or forces are envisioned and experienced is different for each individual Witch, and one might have very different things to say than another about the very same deity, for example.

Nonetheless, it's possible to provide a brief overview about the types of non-physical forces and/or beings commonly found in the traditions of the "Old Religion," as well as in contemporary Witchcraft.

SPIRITS

As discussed above, the animistic worldview sees animals and inanimate objects as being imbued with spirits.

But spirits can also exist on their own, without inhabiting a physical form. They may reside in, or be attached to, a particular place, such as a forest or valley, or they may be free floating, i.e. able to be found anywhere, indoors or out.

A spirit may have once been in human form, as in the spirit of a deceased loved one or ancestor. In fact, some Witches hold that all spirits were once in human form, just as we become spirits when we leave our physical bodies.

Others, however, see a more complex spiritual system in which entities that have never been human are considered to be spirits.

One such category of non-human spirits is the "Elementals," who reside in nature and take many different forms, depending on the particular element they are associated with.

Elementals of Earth are known variously as gnomes, elves, trolls, and/or faeries, depending on the culture and/or region the lore of these beings originates from. Air Elementals are usually referred to as sylphs, though some belief systems include winged faeries in this category as well. Fire Elementals are often called salamanders, and Elementals of water are known as undines, though mermaids and water nymphs are also recognized in this group of water spirits.

These entities can be perceived in nature by those who believe in them and can still their own minds enough to notice their presence. Sylphs may be felt in a particular breeze, while undines might "appear" as a sudden wave rising in an otherwise calm lake.

Witches who work with Elementals may call on them to assist with particular magical purposes aligned with their element.

For example, a candle spell might be augmented with the help of a fire spirit, whose presence may be perceived in the flickering of the candle flame. In the same vein, a faerie spirit might be invoked to help with a working involving stones or herbs.

However, it's generally understood that not all Elementals are necessarily willing to assist human beings, and some may actually be hostile. Offerings to spirits can help foster a positive working relationship with some spirits—and that is indeed often how Witches come to find an affinity with a particular spirit entity—but it should never be assumed that just because a spirit can be perceived and communicated with, that this is going to work out well for the person.

In the realms that Elementals inhabit, the concerns of human beings may seem trivial, laughable, or even annoying. So it's considered unwise to take the good will of these beings for granted.

In fact, it's important to recognize that not all spirits—Elemental or otherwise—are necessarily benevolent, although many certainly are. Some are simply indifferent, or neutral, when it comes to interaction with human beings. Others, however—particularly those regarded as "lower order" spirits—can be actively negative and even harmful toward those in the physical realm.

It has been theorized, for example, that people who suffer from schizophrenia and other psychiatric maladies are ultra-sensitive to the energies of lower order spirits, who enjoy bothering them with severely negative feelings, irrational fears, and other problematic thoughts that keep them from being able to function successfully in everyday "consensual" reality. While these cases may be extreme, it is possible for spiritual energy to cause issues for anyone sensitive enough to perceive it.

To avoid any harmful or unpleasant consequences, it's important for Witches and others who work in the "paranormal" realms to use caution by way of grounding, centering, and shielding techniques to make sure nothing uninvited makes it into their personal space.

As Witches become more adept at working with entities in the spirit world, they may come to discover and develop a relationship with a "spirit guide," one particular spirit who accompanies them throughout their lives and assists with various life challenges, and may also aid in magical work.

This spirit may or may not have ever been incarnated as a human, but will take interest in the Witch's affairs and well-being, communicating through subtle and not-so-subtle ways, such as sounds or scents that seem to come from nowhere, and other seemingly inexplicable phenomena.

The "spirit guide" is not a concept unique to Witchcraft, actually, but is found in many belief systems, and several "New Age" thinkers believe that everyone on the planet has a spirit guide helping them, whether they know it or not. For their part, Witches tend to have an easier time discovering and communicating with their spirit guides, without needing assistance from a medium or other psychic, as many non-Witches might.

Somewhat similar to spirit guides are "familiar spirits," often referred to simply as "familiars."

While belief in spirit guides is widespread across many spiritual and religious systems, the lore around familiars is specific to Witchcraft in the European traditions, and dates back to medieval times.

Familiars were said to be entities that assisted Witches in their magic, and could take various animal forms or even appear to look like humans, but were generally invisible in the physical realm.

Of course, much of the literature regarding familiars was written from a Christian point of view, with information largely gathered from Witch trials in England and Scotland, so they are often portrayed as malevolent, "demon"-like beings, and it's difficult to get an objective sense of the beliefs and practices of those who worked with familiars in those days.

Nonetheless, some contemporary Witches have adopted the concept of familiars, often seeing them in the form of animals. These may be wild animals that come across their paths, such as a crow flying overhead to signal a warning, or even their pets (cats, of course, are very popular familiars for Witches), who can pick up signals from the unseen realms and communicate to their human companions when something strange is afoot.

Alternatively, Witches might work with the *spirit* of a particular "power animal," often in ways that parallel certain Native American traditions, rather than a living animal who is physically present on Earth.

DEITIES

You might find the terms "spirit" and "deity" used interchangeably in sources on Witchcraft, and even by some Witches, who don't recognize any difference between the two.

While it's essentially impossible to categorize non-physical entities in a nice and neat way that satisfies all involved, it's generally acknowledged that spirits and deities are not exactly one and the same.

For example, many spirits do not have names, or at least not that are known to those humans who perceive them. A spirit may only be perceived and recognized by one or two people who live or spend time in the area where the spirit resides, unknown to any other living person in the world.

Deities, by contrast, have names, and are generally recognized by entire communities. Shrines, temples, and other physical structures are erected to honor them. They figure into the mythology of the culture they belong to, often having distinct personalities and stories associated with them.

No one really knows how a deity becomes part of a culture's worldview. The mythology surrounding the pantheons of ancient cultures, such as the Greeks, Romans, Celts, and Germanic tribes came from oral traditions, passed down over centuries with no single author or otherwise traceable source. The same is true of the stories of indigenous cultures around the world.

While every belief system has its origin myth(s) identifying the beings who first created the world, and stories of how later deities emerged to join the pantheon, there's no answer to the question of who or what existed *before* the beginning of a given culture's story, just as there's no answer to that question in the Judeo-Christian creation myth.

But there's certainly no question that for billions of people on the planet today, one or more deities are very real indeed, and their perceptions of these deities shape their culture and the way they approach their lives.

It has been said that deities eventually arose out of animism, as tribal people began to shift into agricultural lifestyles. As their cultures became more complex, they gradually developed ways of organizing their perceptions of the unseen forces at work in their daily lives.

Deities were more than "spirits" of the sky, land, and water—they became associated with particular aspects of life, such as the harvest, healing, and war. Some widely known examples from the ancient Greek world are Artemis, goddess of the hunt, Dionysus, the god of wine, and Apollo, god of poetry and music.

Of course, not all deities were so "specialized" in terms of human civilization—all the while there were still deities associated with specific aspects of nature—the sea, lightning, etc., and countless regional or local deities that had names, dwelling places, and purposes that are now lost to history.

Some Witches understand deities more as "archetypes" than as actual entities or beings.

This doesn't make them any less real, in that they are essentially collections of non-physical energy made more powerful by the consistently reinforced belief and attention of many people. If thought is energy, and thought creates reality—a concept we will explore in more detail below—then it follows that thought creates and sustains deities as a reality.

This perception of deity is often somewhat different from the perception of a spirit, which can be more viscerally felt as a presence in the Witch's vicinity. However, other Witches experience the deities of their practice in very intense and personal ways, and these relationships with deity may be exactly like someone else's experience of spirit guides or Elementals.

Either way, deities may be called upon in magical work, and/or simply revered by Witches, especially Wiccans.

The choice of deity may be based on the particular aim of the magic—the Hindu goddess Lakshmi for prosperity spells or the Celtic god Dagda for protection—or the Witch may have an ongoing, "all-purpose" relationship with a specific, patron deity, an unnamed, all-encompassing Goddess and God, or both.

THE OTHERWORLD

Perhaps because, as human beings, we can't really fathom there being no actual *place* for the unseen entities to inhabit, cultures around the globe have a concept of a world, or worlds, where spirits and deities exist.

This world may be perceived as being above the Earth, below it, all around it, or even coexisting somehow within physical reality.

This world is usually thought to be the place where human spirits go when they leave their physical bodies—either temporarily, through shamanic trance states, or permanently, through death.

For Witches practicing European-based Witchcraft, this world may be referred to as the Otherworld, the Other Side, the Spirit World, Summerland, or a host of other names.

What these worlds look like, feel like, and consist of, and what happens to the spirits of the humans when they arrive there for good depends, of course, on the particular belief system at hand. Some pagan versions of this realm are much more complex than others; some are more pleasant-sounding than others.

As mentioned earlier, some Witches—Wiccans in particular—believe strongly in the "borrowed" concept of reincarnation, while others believe that we permanently inhabit the spirit realm after our human lives, as indicated by the term "afterlife." This fairly important difference tends to shape a Witch's perception of what the spirit realm is like.

Regardless of one's stance on reincarnation, however, Witches who believe in an otherworld seek to interact with it, either through communication with spirits or deities, or actual astral travel to it, in order to gain useful knowledge, work magic, or even commune with the spirits of their departed loved ones.

It might be said by some that this spirit realm is how, and/or where, magical work happens. It can also be said that interacting with this realm is a form of magic itself.

NON-DEIST PANTHEISM

Not all Witches would say they believe in animism, spirits, or deities.

Instead, some experience the non-physical phenomena of magic as an interaction with a single source of energy that exists in equal measure in absolutely everything in the Universe.

This idea is found in many ancient Asian traditions, as well as some slightly more recent Western philosophies. Some names for this energy include All That Is, Akasha, Source, the One, or simply the Universe.

For these Witches, this one source is sufficient as assistance in magic and benevolent guidance through life, so no spirit guides or deities are necessary.

They may also dismiss the idea of an Otherworld or any other type of afterlife, believing instead that the body and spirit simply return to the source as pure energy without retaining an individual identity or personality.

Still others acknowledge this universal force but see it as working through, or manifesting as, spirits and/or entities. They inhabit both perspectives, understanding the power of connection with All That Is, but also feeling a real connection with the ways of the "Old Religion"—as these beliefs are the closest we can get to how the earliest humans would have perceived the Universe.

In other words, they are the closest we can get to the origins of our experience of existence as a species.

ATHEIST WITCHCRAFT: HERMETICISM AND QUANTUM PHYSICS

There are, of course, Witches who do not subscribe to any of the beliefs covered above.

In fact, a significant number of Witches identify as atheists, or secular humanists, and base their belief in magic on an understanding of what they consider rational, rather than "irrational" ideas about the way the world works.

Instead of calling on spirits or deities, or just taking it "on blind faith" that their magic will work, atheist Witches rely on a fundamental principle: that all matter—both visible and invisible—is interconnected, because all matter is essentially *energy* at its core.

This interconnectedness is what makes possible the transformation, or manifestation, of desire into reality.

This scientific concept has gained a wider understanding in recent decades thanks to the growth and development of quantum physics, but it has also been expressed in various terms by mystics, philosophers, and other explorers of mysterious phenomena for thousands of years.

THE HERMETIC PRINCIPLES

Hermeticism is defined as a tradition of philosophical and religious beliefs dating back to antiquity, which are based on a body of writings attributed to Hermes Trismegistus, a supposed priest of the Egyptian god Toth who was said to have written his works sometime before 300 B.C.

There has been much scholarly debate about whether the works are really quite that old (some put them in the first few centuries A.D., instead), as well as about whether Hermes Trismegistus was truly a person, or actually a deity to whom anonymous authors gave the credit for their ideas.

As with many uncertainties about the ancient past, the answers to these questions may never be known, but what is clear is that the ideas attributed to this figure have had significant influence on Western religious, philosophical, scientific and esoteric thinkers over the centuries, including early Christian writers, Isaac Newton, and the founding members of the Hermetic Order of the Golden Dawn.

Although Hermeticism can certainly be called a spiritual tradition, much of it is also compatible with an atheist worldview, in that there is no entity or separate force of any kind that is held responsible for the creation of our world.

A key piece of this wisdom tradition is the collection of seven Hermetic Principles (sometimes called the Hermetic Laws), which describe different ways in which everything in the Universe functions.

These principles are outlined and explained in the *Kybalion*, a book published anonymously in 1908, which sought to bring the teachings of Hermes Trismegistus to a modern audience.

While it has been pointed out that the text is definitely influenced by later occult theory, the Hermetic Principles themselves as laid out in the *Kybalion* are consistent with older works in the Hermetic tradition.

The Hermetic Principles are a key part of the Western Mystery Tradition and are studied and employed by many contemporary Witches—atheists and spiritualists alike.

Below, we'll introduce the first three of the seven principles, which are considered by many Witches to be the most fundamental to understanding the mechanics of magic.

THE PRINCIPLE OF MENTALISM

As stated in the *Kybalion*, this principle asserts that "The All is Mind; The Universe is Mental." Another way to say this is that all matter in the Universe is, at its most basic level, information, or consciousness.

Hermeticism holds that the source of this consciousness is the Universal mind, where all creation stems from.

Consciousness—including conscious thought—is energy, and it creates, through the form of inspiration, the manifestation of inventions, works of art—everything we produce in our world. Magic can be thought of as a particular, focused way of bringing about circumstances we are inspired to create in our lives. We use our conscious thoughts to direct our intentions for desired results.

When we talk about the subconscious mind, we're not talking about non-thought, but about thought that takes place outside the radar of the ego, or the "rational" self. The subconscious mind is an important reservoir and conduit of thought energy, which together with the conscious mind interacts with the Universe as an exchange of energy, sending and receiving information in a constant feedback-loop that facilitates our co-creation with the Universe.

The quality of the manifestation of our co-creation depends in large part on the quality of the thought energy we send out (and we are always co-creating our reality, whether we are aware of it or not), so an awareness of one's emotions and intentions is important to successful magic.

Positive thought energy, which goes hand-in-hand with positive emotion, can manifest desired results. Negative thought energy, on the other hand, is likely to produce either an undesired version of the stated intent, or nothing at all.

The Principle of Mentalism can also be applied to the concept of spirits, in that they exist as consciousness and therefore can communicate with our conscious minds, if we are receptive to their energy. Likewise, we can see the emergence of deities as collections of directed thought that eventually became specified into distinct beings or entities.

But whether Witches work with spirits and/or deities, or are strictly atheists in their view of such phenomena, they are always aware that their thought energy is paramount to co-creating with the mind of the Universal All.

THE PRINCIPLE OF CORRESPONDENCE

The *Kybalion*'s wording of the Principle of Correspondence is "As above, so below; as below so above." Another way to say this is that what is true of the Universe, or the macrocosm, is true of our earthly physical plane, or the microcosm. The higher planes of existence influence the lower planes of existence, and vice versa.

The *Kybalion* uses the idea of "The Three Great Planes," in which one plane is physical, one is mental, and the final plane is spiritual.

However, the text goes on to explain that this is a rough and rather arbitrary categorization, since there is actually no division between the "planes" at the most fundamental level of existence.

Rather than being distinctly separate, they are said to "shade into each other." But it can be useful as a way of understanding that there is as much reality in the "unseen" as there is in what we can observe in our experience in any given moment.

In fact, it could be said that there's far more reality in the unseen, as the unseen contains all of the potential not yet manifested in a given moment.

Witches often use the phrase "as above, so below" as a way of remembering that their intentions are already manifest in the unseen, "non-physical" plane, and therefore must come into being on the physical plane in keeping with the Principle of Correspondence. Once the change has been made through intention in the non-physical plane, the change works its way through the linear time and space of the material plane until it is manifested.

Taken to its logical conclusion in the era of modern physics, the Principle of Correspondence also means that every particle of matter contains all others.

While this can be a difficult concept to wrap the mind around in a visual way, it helps if you remember that the view from the human experience is extremely limited. The physical plane and the linear time we inhabit represent only one dimension in the ultimately infinite and timeless Universe.

Understanding that the Universe is truly limitless, and that, as part of the Universe, our potential is also limitless, helps the more skeptical would-be magician to suspend disbelief enough to work successful magic.

THE PRINCIPLE OF VIBRATION

Just as all matter is essentially information, matter is also in constant motion in the form of vibration. Nothing is ever at rest, at the basic level of energy, no matter how much a given object may appear to be perfectly still.

Objects that we experience as stationary and solid are simply vibrating at a much, much lower frequency than we can perceive from our human perspective.

When we add this Principle of Vibration to those of Mentalism and Correspondence, we can understand that the differences between the "planes" of existence are simply different vibrational frequencies of the same source—or mind—that gives rise to everything in the Universe.

This principle has an interesting correlation with the concept of animism, in that it recognizes no fundamental distinction between "living" and "non-living" when it comes to material phenomena.

The state of being that we would define as physically "alive" is simply a particular frequency of vibration. The state of being that we would define as "deceased" is simply a different frequency.

Those who believe that we do not cease to exist when we die are drawing on the understanding, consciously or unconsciously, that a higher vibrational frequency is involved in the transition from "physical" body to "non-physical" spirit.

But whether or not one's understanding of the Principle of Vibration incorporates a concept of an afterlife, it's clear that we can feel the motion, or vibration, of invisible phenomena.

All day long, we can feel thoughts moving through our minds, and even those that seem to be "stuck" in our minds are actually moving around over and over again, often creating unpleasantness.

Witches know that approaching magical work without a clear, well-focused and intentioned mindset is unlikely to produce results, since the vibrational frequency of unpleasant or otherwise distracting thoughts muddies up the work.

The particular vibrational frequency of the Witch is more important than any individual ingredient in a spell, which is why many will make use of meditation and visualization techniques before beginning any spellwork.

So here we have another way of seeing how thought, or intent, is the engine behind magical manifestation, as it vibrates in interaction with the rest of the Universe.

OTHER COMPONENTS
OF THE HERMETIC SYSTEM

Of the seven Hermetic Principles, Mentalism, Correspondence, and Vibration are probably the most helpful and relevant to the foundations of most types of magic.

The other four principles, Polarity, Rhythm, Cause and Effect, and Gender, are also worth exploring for those interested in learning more about this framework for understanding the Universe.

Furthermore, there is a related concept, widely known as the "Law of Attraction," which has received much attention in the past couple of decades. It is described in *the Kybalion* as one way in which the Law of Correspondence functions—it brings about "as above, so below" in the form of "like attracts like."

In this framework, positive thoughts attract positive experiences because the person having the thoughts is vibrating at the right frequency to attract the positive experiences. Magic can be used to improve one's emotional frequency—as in a spell for emotional healing—in order to work with the Law of Attraction in a way that brings, or "attracts," desired results.

SCIENCE CATCHES UP WITH THE "OLD RELIGION"

Although today's scientific community might not like to acknowledge their link with Hermeticism due to its association with spirituality and the occult, the truth is that the forefathers of what we now recognize as the scientific tradition were students of it.

From Copernicus to Francis Bacon, the great thinkers who brought the scientific method into widespread use were applying the insights of Hermeticism in their experiments. So it comes as no surprise to those who understand the Hermetic Principles that modern science is continuing to validate them, with a new vocabulary and framework for explaining the fundamental workings of the Universe.

The field of science that is currently most resonant with the ideas discussed above is variously referred to as quantum mechanics, quantum physics, and/or quantum theory.

This branch of physics, like Hermeticism, is concerned with understanding the makeup of the Universe at its most basic level—in the form of subatomic particles.

Among some of the discoveries within this leading edge field of study are that the interaction between particles transcends time and space altogether, and that reality as we know it is shaped by how we perceive it.

It's beyond the scope of this guide to go into detail about the tenets of quantum theory or its many components, but readers who are scientifically inclined will find the parallels with Hermeticism and other occult ideas very interesting indeed.

THE UNIFIED FIELD

One particular parallel, which is related to quantum mechanics but ultimately predates it, is found in unified field theory.

Sometimes called the "Theory of Everything," this scientific line of inquiry seeks to understand the nature and behavior of all existence as interconnected by a single "field," or controlling force.

The origins of this theory go back to the mid-nineteenth century, and it was brought to widespread public attention through the work of Einstein, who coined the term "unified field theory," as he was attempting to reconcile seemingly incompatible or opposing physical phenomena.

But while much progress has been made in this cutting-edge branch of physics, scientists have yet to work out a truly comprehensive theory of "everything." (Witches, on the other hand, can make use of the concept without needing to have all of the details worked out in a nice, neat, "rational" manner.)

The premise of unified field theory is that the Universe, at its most fundamental level, is made up of four types of interactions. These are electromagnetism, gravity, strong force interaction, and weak force interaction.

Many thinkers whose ideas bridge both science and spirituality have observed that the unified field tying these interactions together is actually a conscious energy field, where thought, or intent, drives creation. Again, a full explanation of unified field theory is beyond the scope of this guide, but glimmers of evidence for the conscious energy field can be seen in various seemingly mysterious phenomena.

Two examples are found in the recent discoveries of "social networking" among different plant species, and of interactions between thought forms and water molecules.

Biologists have been deepening their understanding of plant behavior through experiments that show plants to have far more sensory experience than previously thought. They respond to their environment in ways that go far beyond simply growing taller in good sunlight—they also actively avoid predators and have sense memories around threatening encounters with human beings.

In a forest setting, it has been observed that plants will interact with each other by exchanging nutrients through a network of underground fungi. In essence, various species are able to communicate with each other through chemical "signals" in order to work together for the optimal survival of the entire forest "network."

But perhaps a more widely known, and certainly more observable, example of the ultimate interconnectedness of the Universe is the set of experiments conducted by Dr. Masaro Emoto, described in his book series *The Hidden Messages of Water*.

In these experiments, water molecules were shown to change their basic structure in response to different emotional messages communicated by both spoken and written words.

Molecules exposed to positive messaging formed beautiful crystalline structures when viewed in frozen form under a microscope, while molecules exposed to negative messaging formed misshapen, incomplete crystals.

Both of these discoveries seem fairly astonishing, but when viewed in the context of the unified field of consciousness, or even the Principle of Mentalism, perhaps they shouldn't be.

CONCEPTS AND USES OF MAGIC IN THE MODERN WORLD

As you can see by now, there are a variety of beliefs, worldviews, and even examples of "scientific evidence" that Witches may draw from in their practice of the Craft.

Whether they work with deities, other entities from the spirit world, the unified field of consciousness, or simply "energy," Witches work by harnessing the power available to them and connecting it with their own in order to manifest change.

And although the word "magic" has been rather distorted in the way it's been used and defined over the centuries, to the point where it seems impossible to separate it from fantasy, it still seems to be the closest word we can find to describe what it is that Witches are capable of.

The word "magic" in English dates back to the late 14th century, when it was adapted from the Old French word "magique." In those days, the word was defined as "the art of influencing events and producing marvels using hidden natural forces."

By contrast, a contemporary definition calls magic "the power of apparently influencing the course of events by using mysterious or supernatural forces."

The words "apparently" and "supernatural" show how the mainstream culture's view of magic has shifted since the scientific revolution first took hold. Because magic cannot be proven according to any scientific understanding of the laws of nature, it's dismissed out of hand as not being real. But Witches know very well that the original definition of magic still holds.

It's also interesting that in this shift of definitions, the concept of magic went from being an *art* to a *power*.

Most Witches will agree that magic is an art, and that while "power" (or energy) is involved, this power doesn't come solely from the individual. The power, whether you understand it in terms of the functions described in Hermeticism, or unified field theory, or the infinite ways of spirit world, is all around us. And for most Witches, this power is most easily found and accessed through interaction with nature.

They know that the natural world is still our original home, no matter how "civilized" we may have become, and so they pay close attention to it, observing the ongoing process of creation, destruction, and change and attuning to those energies in their work.

This can mean honoring and working in harmony with seasonal changes and phases of the moon, utilizing the innate properties of the four elements, and/or drawing on the subtle energies of crystals and herbs to enhance the power of their intentions.

In this light, perhaps a more accurate definition of magic would be "the process and the results that occur from consciously participating in the co-creative forces of the Universe by using the subtle energies of nature to cause desired change in one's reality."

NATURE AS CO-CREATOR

Most of us have seen at least one "magic show" where a skilled stage magician, or illusionist, will perform a sleight-of-hand trick of some kind with the help of a "trusty assistant."

When it comes to actual magic, nature is the trusty assistant, helping the practitioner achieve the aim through a combination of cyclical rhythm, elemental forces, and physical tools.

It's interesting to note that the forbears of Witchcraft—the cunning folk, soothsayers, and shamans of prior centuries—probably didn't put the kind of emphasis on the concept of nature as modern Witches do.

Before the industrial revolution, most people lived a very rural life, tied intricately with nature, and so had no need to remember to get "back" to it. These days, connecting with nature does seem to require more of a conscious effort, especially for Witches living hectic lives in urban areas.

Luckily, the aspects of nature that Witches commune with are eternal, and so have been here all along, available to anyone wishing to tune into the natural world and work within the context of its many relationships, and its infinite power.

Perhaps the most fundamental relationship in nature, at least from a human perspective, is that between the Earth and the Sun. Without the Sun, of course, life on Earth could not exist. And it's the Earth's orbit around the Sun that causes seasons to occur.

Furthermore, the plant and animal life found in any given place on Earth will depend on that place's relationship to this orbit as the Earth turns on its axis. For example, whales and seals evolved to thrive in the polar regions, where the warmth from the Sun's light is at its weakest, while all kinds of reptiles are found at the equator, where the Sun's warmth is consistently very strong.

While plenty of other factors influence the diversity of life on Earth, the Sun is the primary catalyst. So it's a very logical place to start when it comes to how Witches might time their magic.

For example, the equinoxes and solstices (sometimes called the "solar holidays"), are considered to be particularly powerful times of the year to honor and appreciate the Sun and to work magic.

The Autumn and Spring Equinoxes favor intentions for balance, since they occur at the exact midpoints of the Earth's yearly orbit, when the days and nights are of equal length. The Winter Solstice marks the beginning of the return of the waxing light, and so is considered a time to plant intentions for the coming year. The Summer Soltsice is an opportunity to celebrate the high point of the growing season, thank the Sun for its light and the life it gives rise to, and to begin focusing energy on "harvesting" results of magical efforts.

All four of these points around the "wheel of the year" provide time to pause and reflect on both the temporary and cyclical nature of our experience on Earth.

The Moon is just as important when it comes to magical timing. In fact, for many Witches, its power and influence is actually more significant than the Sun's, due to its gravitational pull on the Earth—which creates the ocean tides—and its effects on the human psyche and even the human body.

Phases of the moon's cycle are considered to be very influential on the outcome of spellwork, so that working with the waxing moon is beneficial for magic involving increasing something in one's life, while the waning moon is best for decrease, or letting go of something in one's life.

Likewise, the Full Moon is considered to have an amplifying effect on magic, while the New Moon is considered a good time for giving magic a rest, or else focusing on inward-directed work, such as strengthening psychic skills.

Many Witches work with one or more of the four elements—earth, air, fire, and water—in their spellcraft.

The recognition of these "classical" elements in the Western Mystery Tradition comes from the ancient Greeks, who believed that these four natural phenomena were the basic building blocks of all matter.

We have seen, in Part Two of this guide, that Wiccan ritual usually involves an invocation of the elements, and that Elemental spirit beings might be a part of the belief system of Wiccan and non-Wiccan Witches alike. Beyond these practices, however, there are other ways of incorporating the elements in magical work, including choosing an element that's particularly suited to the aim of the work.

For example, fire is the great transformer, so spells for change may involve writing what one wants to change on a piece of paper and burning it in the flame of a candle or even an outdoor fire. Water, on the other hand, is healing and soothing, which makes a healing ritual bath incredibly powerful. Workings for balance, whether in physical well-being or in some other aspect of life, might involve representations of all four of the elements together.

Finally, nature provides the Witch with a wide array of tools for magic and ritual, whether it's a wand made from a slender branch of elm or a pinch of dried thyme to use in a spell for increased courage.

As we've seen above, not all Witches incorporate ritual tools into their practice. In fact, there is quite a wide spectrum in this department, from those who prefer the elaborately laid altar with ornately-carved chalice and pentacle, etc. to the Witch who relies on nothing but the power of her own focused mind.

For those Witches who do work with tools, however, and particularly those who fall into the "Green Witchery" category, nature has plenty to offer in the form of plant life, rocks and crystals, water streams and rivers, and pure, simple soil.

AIMS OF MAGIC

Over the centuries, Witches worked magic for an untold variety of purposes, whether for personal gain, on behalf of family or neighbors, or on behalf of paying customers.

In some sense, not much has changed.

Contemporary magic is by and large focused on improving one's own circumstances, perhaps most often in matters of health, wealth, and love. Protection is another common aim of magic, whether it's physical or emotional protection, or guarding against negative energy of some kind. And for those Witches who consider themselves spiritual, or even religious beings, magic and spiritual development go hand in hand.

Witches also work on behalf of others in today's world, including friends and family, and some in the Craft do work for others who pay for their services.

Indeed, the "Witch business" is alive and well on the Internet, with offerings ranging from magical herbs to specially charged potions and charm bags, and even full-blown custom spellwork on the behalf of the client.

But a great many Witches also work for the wider good of their communities and the world, sending intentions for the healing of the environment, an end to poverty, and other global concerns.

One contemporary tradition of Witchcraft is the Reclaiming tradition, which emerged in the U.S. in the 1970s out of influences from the Feri and Dianic traditions, and specifically emphasizes environmental responsibility, working for social equality and community well-being.

In the age of the Internet, as globalization continues to create an unprecedented sense of world community, there is more opportunity than ever for those in the Craft to join their energies with each other and with the world's other "intention workers"—such as the Buddhist monks who collectively meditate for world peace— in the effort to solve global problems.

Many Witches are choosing to heed that call, both in coven work and in solitary practice.

However, not all who work with the "hidden forces of nature" are necessarily concerned with the collective greater good. Witches are a diverse bunch, and a desire to be of service to others is not a requirement for practicing the Craft.

Indeed, people come to Witchcraft for all kinds of reasons, with a broad spectrum of perspectives about what magic is for. Before moving on to a more specific discussion of magical aims and methods, it's worth a closer look at the question of magical motives.

WITCHCRAFT AND ETHICS

As discussed in Part Two, there is a significant difference of opinion, particularly between Wiccans and Traditional Witches, about whether or not magic should only be used for "positive" purposes.

At the heart of the Wiccan philosophy of magic is the rule of "an it harm none, do what ye will," often expressed simply as "harm to none" (or "the Rede," in acknowledgement of the source of the phrase).

This rule has both an ethical basis and a purely pragmatic one.

Wiccans see themselves as ethical people with compassion for others, who would never willfully cause harm in another's life—or at least they strive to live this way.

And if the temptation to seek control through manipulative magic should arise, the pragmatic part of the rule kicks in to remind them that whatever they send out into the Universe will come back to them.

(And those who believe in the Threefold Law have three times more reason not to engage in malevolent magic of any kind!)

This is a form of what some call "instant karma," which most people, in or out of the Craft, have experienced at some point in their lives, whether they recognized it as such or not.

It's worth a reminder here that there are plenty of non-Wiccan Witches who follow "harm to none" in their own way, but they may or may not distinguish between "positive" and "negative" magic.

Again, this is due to differing concepts of what magic really is and how or why it works. But one's perspective on this question of "harm to none" can also depend on how well the history of Witchcraft in the Western world is understood.

WITCHES WERE NEVER SAINTS

Among many Wiccans and other believers in "positive magic only," there is a kind of idealist view of history that portrays the Witches of the past as completely innocent victims of persecution for their beliefs and practices.

Many Wiccan writers tend to mislead their audiences about the era of European witch-hunts and their resulting trials and executions—often referred to as "the burning times"—both through exaggeration and selective detail. They paint a portrait of masses of brutish Christians indiscriminately punishing millions of people who believed and practiced outside of the "true religion" of Christianity.

While these unfortunate events certainly took place, they did not number in the millions, as some Witches claim. Instead, historians place the actual estimate between the thousands and tens of thousands.

This is not to argue that anyone killed or otherwise punished for being a Witch deserved their fate, but to point out that this portrayal of the past tends to whitewash a rather undeniable fact: Witchcraft *was* used for both benevolent and malevolent purposes.

Why else would we have the terms "white witch" "dark witch," or "black witch"? Or distinctions between "witches" and "cunning folk," which are found across European cultures, including those of England, France, Italy, and Scandinavia? And let's keep in mind that there were also unscrupulous "cunning folk" who were sometimes known to cast the very curses or hexes that they were later paid to lift!

Indeed, there is an incredible amount of lore regarding the malicious deeds and capabilities of those labeled as "witches" in prior centuries, some of which is quite disturbing to some.

Witches were said to make farm animals sicken and die, curse field crops, and bring all other sorts of bad fortune. They might do these things for hire, or out of personal spite toward their victims.

There was also plenty of belief in the ability to summon "demons" and other forms of malevolent spiritual energy, which the Witch might engage in just for the sheer fun of it.

It's true that these stories are written from a biased, anti-pagan, Christian point of view, and that much of it seems exaggerated and even preposterous to contemporary minds, such as the common tale of the Witch turning people into toads. It's also true that, as discussed in Part One of this guide, lack of knowledge of the physical causes of disease, crop failure, and the like led to suspicions of malicious spellwork that most likely did not take place.

Nonetheless, it's still not useful to pretend that *all* practitioners of the Craft were completely ethical and compassionate in their work at all times. Curses and hexes exist, and their history is just as old as any other type of magical work.

Many non-Wiccan Witches assert that it's important to have as accurate a portrayal as possible of the history of Witchcraft, even when it means acknowledging the uglier parts.

After all, our ancestors in the Craft tradition were human beings, just like us, with the capacity for anger, jealousy, the desire to manipulate others, and other unpleasant traits, and so it should come as no surprise that methods for acting on those motivations were, and still are, as well-practiced as any healing, blessing, or other work motivated by our better natures.

BLACK AND WHITE MAGIC

Indeed, if you run a search on "black magic" on the Internet, you will find plenty of sites and authors that plainly describe, defend, and even advocate for using this type of work.

Spells for revenge are common, as are manipulative love spells. You can also find spells to break up a marriage, or to cause serious illness, or even death!

Most of this information is offered with stern warnings about the energetic (or "karmic") consequences of such workings, and some of these writers state that the spells are *only* for informative purposes and should never actually be tried.

But others seem to believe that there are plenty of times when black magic is justified.

In fact, some are simply not troubled by a sense of "conscience" and see life as a sort of amoral "eat or be eaten" experience, where strength and power at all costs are paramount to success. These practitioners could be said to be on the opposite end of the spectrum from those Witches who not only practice "harm to none," but also direct their energies toward improving things for others.

As for the notion of "black" and "white" magic, it should be pointed out that Witches who don't perceive a distinction between "positive" and "negative" magic also disagree with these terms. They believe that since all energy is inherently neutral, the vibrational frequency of every color can be put to use for good or harm.

Magic making use of the color black can be used for protection or to increase personal power in the pursuit of a goal, just as the color white could be used in an ill-intentioned working. It's *how* colors are used that determines their effect. In other words, the distinction is really about the intent of the practitioner when working the spell, as opposed to the type of energy being used.

From this perspective, magic that causes an unwanted effect in another person's life can be justified if the intent is in the best interest of the person casting the spell. For example, protecting oneself from an abusive person might necessarily result in a negative experience coming to that person that prevents them from doing further harm.

If the intent is one of self-protection, rather than retaliation for something the other person did, then this kind of magic can be described as "neutral," rather than harmful or manipulative. The spellwork is seen as merely a tool for achieving a necessary aim, just as a spell for getting a new job or healing from an illness would be.

THE ENERGY OF INTENTION

Still, it can be argued that the specific *type* of magic chosen for accomplishing the aim will have a particular effect on the Witch who casts the spell.

As mentioned earlier, the principle of the Return of Energy means that whatever one sends out into the Universe will come back, often in unexpected ways. So if Witches are in the habit of sending out direct intentions to create harmful circumstances, such as in the form of hexes or curses as a means of self-protection, it's likely that they're inviting more situations into their lives that call for *needing* self-protection.

This is an example of the Law of Attraction at work: whatever we focus on brings more of it into our lives, so it makes more practical sense to find ways to work in a manner that causes harm to none.

In our self-protection example, this can be done through a magical severing of the energetic connection between the Witch and the threatening person, with no attachment to what happens to that person as a result.

This guide recommends this latter approach to "harm to none" when it comes to dealing with negative circumstances in magic.

Working from a neutral standpoint is ideal here, as it is bound to bring much better results for the Witch in the long term. As for all other situations, working from as positive a place as possible has been shown to have the most impact on a person's life.

For example, if you're trying to get a promotion at your job, it's not wise to intend for someone else to be fired in order to make it happen. You're better off simply visualizing yourself in the position you want to be in, with the intention of harm to none, and then letting the Universe work out how it happens.

A CLOSER LOOK

We've now examined a number of common beliefs, practices, and attitudes surrounding the use of magic in contemporary Witchcraft.

Of course, this is only a brief look into each of these areas, and interested readers can find more extensive information on everything discussed above. There are entire books on working with deities, the wisdom of Hermeticism, the role of the moon in magic, and just about any other topic related to Witchcraft. You'll find a brief list of references at the end of this guide to get you started.

Part Four, the final section of this guide, will serve as a brief introduction to the hands-on practice of magic.

We'll examine a few common forms of magic that are particularly good for developing mindfulness skills that, over time and with practice, can greatly increase a Witch's success.

For those who've been curious about trying magic for themselves, the activities here are a great way to take the next step along your path.

PART FOUR

EXPLORING YOUR INNER WITCH

GETTING STARTED

Just like Witchcraft, magic itself takes an enormous variety of different forms. Many of these use material tools, while others are strictly "mental," relying on the Witch's powers of intentional, focused concentration.

Actually, many Witches would consider *all* directed intention to be part of magic, even if it's just sending a good thought to a friend who pops into the mind while one is doing dishes.

As mentioned in Part Two, Kitchen and Green Witches will send intentions, or direct magical energy, into the herbs and flowers they plant & grow, and into the soups and baked goods they create for themselves and loved ones. Indeed, far from being a hobby or a separate activity outside of one's normal life, for the long-practicing Witch, magic is really a way of life.

For beginners exploring the rich and diverse world of magical forms and techniques, the options can seem overwhelming.

There's nothing wrong with starting small—in fact, it's really the only way to start.

In this section, we'll cover three different forms of magic— visualization, invocation, and candle magic—with an example working of each that you can try if you'd like.

The first two workings are good for helping yourself get in the right "head space" for an effective magical practice. The third is a simple candle spell that anyone can succeed with, with or without prior magical experience.

Of course, time is still an essential ingredient in all this, so don't be discouraged if you don't feel like something "worked" right away. It may take a few tries to get into the right frame of mind for magic to really start manifesting.

Remember, like all skilled activity, magic takes practice. No one becomes a master manifestor overnight!

CREATIVE VISUALIZATION

If the Universe is ultimately mental, then the use of creative visualization can be seen as a direct interaction with the Universe that manifests a desired result. (This is why it's called *creative*!)

Of course, this ability is not just for Witches—visualization techniques are used in preparation for many different activities, from sports games to business presentations.

In magic, visualization a key part of spellwork success. But it's also useful for tapping into the regions of the mind that are normally dormant during waking consciousness, opening us up to our own creative power.

For many Witches, getting practiced in the art of visualization is not only good for strengthening spellwork, but also for communing with ancestors and deities, or other aspects of spiritual development.

VISUALIZATION FOR ATTUNING TO MAGICAL ENERGY

Below is a meditative visualization that helps you get attuned to (or "in tune with") your own inherent personal power. We have to be connected to the spirit world, or the universal energy, from within ourselves, rather than trying to locate the "magic" in a source outside ourselves.

Practicing this nature-inspired visualization is a great way to create an inner sanctuary for yourself to visit whenever you'd like to reconnect with the energy you find there.

Tip: It can be fairly hard to conduct a successful visualization from written text, particularly since you're unlikely to memorize every detail before beginning. Instead, it's best to listen to this passage being read aloud, either by a friend or from a voice recording. Most smart phones have voice recorder apps built-in, so this can be a fairly easy fix. If you can't find a friend or a voice recorder, then try copying down the visualization by hand—this helps your mind to remember the details better.

For this visualization, as with any other magical working, it's ideal to be alone and in a place you know you won't be disturbed.

****

You are standing at the edge of a very old, thickly wooded forest, facing the trees.

You can see the tall brown trunks of pine trees and the bright green leaves of oaks and maples. The leaves flutter in the breeze and the tallest trunks sway ever so slightly up above.

You can hear the faint stirrings of a stronger wind moving through a deeper part of the forest, and feel a slight, soft rain begin to mist the skin on your cheekbones.

The ground is rocky beneath your shoes.

Before you is a narrow dirt path that leads into the woods.

You take a long, slow, deep breath in and hold it there for a moment, allowing the scent of pine trees to fill your mind.

Exhale slowly, and then step onto the path.

Walk softly, but deliberately, conscious of putting one foot in front of the other, as you continue to listen to the breeze moving through the forest.

Look all around you at the trunks, branches, and leaves of each tree as you pass. Notice the leaf-covered floor of the forest and the shrubs growing in the spaces between the trees.

Trust the path as it leads you deeper into the forest, winding and turning gently, feeling and hearing the small pebbles crunching under your feet.

There's a giant fallen oak lying to the left of you that seems to be pointing toward something beyond your field of vision.

A squirrel runs softly across the length of the trunk, and you follow it with your eyes until it disappears into the depths of the forest.

You keep walking, and slowly the path begins to widen and become smoother, until it it's nothing but soft earth.

As you look up, you see that you have come to a clearing, where blue and violet wildflowers sprout up around a few grey boulders. The clouds overhead scatter and the sun emerges, shining brightly and bathing your skin in golden light.

Sit down in this place.

Take off your shoes and connect your bare feet with the earth. Take a few breaths & feel the vastness of the forest all around you.

The wind has quieted, and birds are reemerging to call out from high branches in the surrounding trees.

You hear a crow caw four times from somewhere above your head, and the flapping of its wings as it departs from its perch and soars away.

In the silence that follows, you become very, very still.

Then, from the corner of your eye, you spot a deer hovering at the edge of the clearing, to your left.

Silently, slowly, you turn your head to face the deer.

She is looking directly at you, and the two of you lock gazes for a moment, as if you are both frozen in time.

Then, the deer steps quietly away. You can hear twigs crackling under her hooves as she disappears from your sight line.

After the deer has made her exit, take a few more deep, peaceful breaths in this clearing.

Then, when you feel ready, slowly allow the room you are in to come back into your awareness.

Begin to release the images in your mind, until you can picture your actual physical surroundings clearly.

Bring your awareness back into your body by wiggling your fingers and toes. When you have completely returned to the room, slowly open your eyes.

You have now invited the hidden energy of spirit into your awareness.

****

After working this visualization, it's a great idea to free-write any thoughts or impressions that occurred to you during the process. So keep a journal or paper and pen nearby.

You can also, during the visualization, ask the deer for a personal message that will come to you in a dream or in some unusual moment in your waking life.

Try practicing this exercise every day for a week. You'll be surprised by how much more in tune you are feeling with your magical energy—that same energy that nudged you to read this guide.

INVOCATION

Invocation is a way of seeking guidance, assistance, and/or connection from a spirit helper, a deity, or other power in the unseen world.

This type of work can take many forms, from simple prayer (which is found in all major religions) to more advanced workings in which one actually allows the energy of the spirit being invoked to enter one's body.

Another form involves summoning a being from the spirit world in order to do one's magical bidding. That kind of magic is fairly advanced, as well as somewhat ethically controversial, given that it creates a hierarchical structure that places the Witch in power over the energy being summoned, which some Witches feel is out of balance.

The form of invocation below, by contrast, is a respectful invitation to the invoked energy to join the Witch as an equal, and to assist, if needed, as a good friend would.

INVOCATION FOR FINDING A SPIRIT HELPER

If you have ever sensed the presence of a benevolent energy around you, but not been quite sure if you were imagining things, this can be a great exercise to try. You may be quite surprised to find you've had a helper in the spirit world all along!

Many people believe we all have spirit helpers whether we are aware of them or not. Others believe we need to actively seek them.

Whatever your beliefs might be, this invocation can be used to connect with an existing spirit helper or to appeal to the spirit world for a new helper.

If you can, you might want to try this right after doing the visualization provided above. In fact, once you've practiced the visualization a few times, you could try working this invocation while you're sitting in the clearing!

Steps:

Sit comfortably alone in a place where you know you won't be disturbed. You might want to play some quiet meditation music or other sounds that help you tune into your inner self.

Ground and center yourself by taking a few long, slow, deep breaths with your eyes closed. When you feel settled and still, speak the following words aloud:

As I sit in my power in the world of form,
I ask the spirit world to greet me in warmth and light.
Guide, I ask you now to come forth and meet me.
Gently make your presence known,
and walk with me on my magical journey.
Thank you for your assistance, now
and in the future. So let it be.

Sit quietly for a few deep breaths after speaking the invocation. Notice any subtle shifts in energy that occur. You may feel warmer or cooler than before, or simply sense that something in and around you has changed.

It can also be good to keep paper and pen handy for this work, as you may very well receive some messages from your spirit helper!

In fact, make it a point to free-write everything that comes to mind for 3 to 10 minutes after working the invocation. After a few tries, you are certain to notice some patterns, either in your physical experience or in the thoughts you're writing down. It can take a while, but the spirit world is definitely answering your invitation!

When you're ready to return to mundane activities, be sure to thank the spirit world for whatever energy and/or messages you've received, and release it back into non-physical form. You can simply say "thank you," take a few deep, grounding breaths, and consciously release the energetic connection.

CANDLE MAGIC

Possibly the most widely practiced form of magic that involves tools, candle magic is very popular with beginners because it's fairly simple, accessible, and easy to learn.

Fire is one of the classical elements, and flames speak to a primal essence in ourselves in a way that facilitates magical transformation.

If you've ever simply watched the flame of a candle wavering on the wick, or the sparks shooting out from embers in a bonfire, you already know the mesmerizing power of fire.

Using this energy to project a specific intention into the unseen world of spirit can be a very effective way of manifesting your desired results.

Don't expect to win the lottery on your first try, however. Your state of mind, your ability to *believe* you will receive what you are seeking, and your ability to let go and trust the Universe are all much more important than the candle or the flame.

And getting into that frame of mind takes practice and discipline.

One way you can enhance your mental powers is to spend some time in meditation before working this (or any other) spell. You might even try preparing for this spell by using the visualization and/or the invocation above first.

However you approach this part of the task is up to you. Just don't expect to be able to come home from a busy day at work and immediately be in the right frame of mind to work magic!

CANDLE SPELL FOR INNER PEACE

Rather than starting off with a spell for a material result, it's good to get a feel for candle magic by working on your own inner state of being.

Spells for improving your emotional or mental state are generally highly effective—in fact, the only way these types of spells can go wrong is if you actively resist the manifestation!

The spell below is for achieving a sense of peace and calm, and is good for any occasion, but it's particularly useful after a period of stress and upheaval, or before an upcoming event that has you feeling anxious.

If you've got an important exam, a job interview, or a dentist appointment that's twisting up your insides, work this spell as often as necessary in the evenings leading up to the dreaded event. You'll find yourself feeling much lighter in general, which will help you meet the challenge with greater success.

You'll need a white candle of any size or shape—white is a color associated with peace, calming, centering, and positive vibrations.

Tea lights or spell candles are optimal, since you can leave these to burn all the way down, which is a recommended practice for many spells, but particularly for your first excursion into candle magic.

However, larger candles will also work, and they give you the opportunity to repeat the spell each night until the candle is completely spent. Choose whichever option feels better according to your own intuition.

Steps:

As you prepare to light your candle, sit and hold it in both hands with eyes closed, breathing slowly and deeply.

Visualize yourself filled with, and surrounded by, glowing white light, and feel yourself relax into this healing vibrational space.

If you're working the spell in advance of a specific occasion, envision yourself *after* the event is over, feeling that sense of relief that comes with getting something scary or otherwise unpleasant out of the way.

You should feel a shift inside yourself as you imagine this moment.

When you're ready, open your eyes, light the candle and say the following words:

> *White light, calm and bright,*
> *thank you for the peace you bring this night.*
> *Peace and calm surround me now,*
> *flowing through me, feet to brow.*
> *I hold it gently through the coming day*
> *as peaceful energy lights my way.*

Sit quietly and gaze at the flame, allowing it to lull you into a deeper sense of calm.

You can repeat the words if you like, as often as it feels useful.

Leave the candle burning at least until you go to bed, and if it's still going then, place it in a sink to finish burning safely.

If it's a larger candle and you need to extinguish it, do so gently, with a snuffer, a soft breath, or waving your hand above the flame. Thank the energy of the fire for its work on your behalf.

You can then repeat the spell again on subsequent evenings, until the candle is spent, or simply call up that sense of inner peace before relighting it for any occasion.

CONTINUING
ON YOUR JOURNEY

Now that you've had a chance to explore just a select few magical techniques and practices, you may be wondering where to go from here.

The most helpful answer to that question is to keep reading as much about the Craft as you can, all the while paying attention to your inner guidance. (You can begin your search for more information with the list of suggested references at the end of this guide.)

As you pursue new knowledge, you will find books and online resources that resonate with you, and others that may seem too "out there," or just not quite your style.

It takes time to identify your own path, so don't be impatient! In fact, most Witches consider the study of the Craft to be a lifelong pursuit, with ongoing learning, experimenting, and refining.

And perhaps most importantly, the journey should be fun!

CONCLUSION

Approaching any kind of religious or spiritual practice for the first time can seem daunting. There's so much to learn, so much available information, and so many differing perspectives on what is "correct" or "incorrect" in terms of knowledge and practice.

As you've seen throughout this guide, Witchcraft is no exception. In fact, it may be the most confounding of all possible areas of spirituality!

The aim of this guide has been to provide a fact-based, neutrally-oriented context for launching you on your study of the Craft. By examining the place Witchcraft occupies in the broader global context of non-monotheistic spirituality, as well as the known and unknown origins of today's various traditions, you should have a better grounding in this fascinating field, and hopefully a clearer sense of where you'd like to go next.

Whether you feel called to study Wicca with a practicing coven, learn as much as you can on your own about a branch of Traditional Witchcraft, or forge an eclectic practice that combines several approaches, you should have a practical grounding that can help you navigate the various opinions, definitions, and perspectives you'll find in the wide, wide world of the Craft.

I'll leave you with one piece of parting advice, though: make sure you stick to your own path. I can't tell you what that is, and perhaps you can't answer with any clarity at this point.

Read, read, and read some more, and at some point you will feel an idea "calling" to you. If an idea resonates with you, it's probably your intuition telling you that this is the direction you're supposed to go—the path you're supposed to take.

And when you have figured out the path you want to take, read, read, and read some more all over again! Continuous learning is one of the best ways to get more from your experiences with Witchcraft.

Remember: Never let anyone tell you what's right or wrong, what you should believe, or which direction you should take. There are no right or wrongs, just different interpretations.

I will leave you with that thought, as it is now time for you to start your own journey, and interpret the information presented to you in your own way. As I've already mentioned, this introductory guide should represent only the starting point in your learning. To help you educate yourself further, I've included a number of useful resources that are well worth a read.

I sincerely hope that you enjoyed learning about Witchcraft with me, as it is a topic close to my heart. Whichever the direction you choose to follow, I wish you all the best on your journey.

Thank you one more time for reading. Blessed Be.

SUGGESTIONS FOR FURTHER READING

The following brief list is classified according to the three main broad categories of contemporary Witchcraft as identified in this guide. Please note that there are many, many more resources available in print and online in addition to these suggestions. Happy reading!

Traditional Witchcraft

Nigel Pennick, *Secrets of East Anglian Magic* (1995)

Gemma Gary, *The Black Toad - West Country Witchcraft and Magic* (2012)

Emma Wilby, *Cunning Folk and Familiar Spirits: Shamanistic Visionary Traditions in Early Modern British Witchcraft and Magic* (2005)

Evan John Jones, Robert Cochrane, and Michael Howard, *The Roebuck in the Thicket: An Anthology of the Robert Cochrane Witchcraft Tradition* (2001)

Wicca

Gerald Gardner, *Witchcraft Today* (1955) and *The Meaning of Witchcraft* (1959)

Doreen Valiente, *Where Witchcraft Lives* (1962)

Raymond Buckland, *Witchcraft....The Religion* (1966)

Scott Cunningham, *Wicca: A Guide for the Solitary Practitioner* (1989)

Eclectic Witchcraft

Ellen Dugan, *Natural Witchery: Intuitive, Personal & Practical Magick* (2007)

Laurie Cabot with Tom Cowan, *Power of the Witch: The Earth, the Moon, and the Magical Path to Enlightenment* (1990)

D.J. Conway, *Celtic Magic* (1990)

THREE FREE
AUDIOBOOKS PROMOTION

Don't forget, you can now enjoy **three audiobooks completely free of charge** when you start a free 30-day trial with Audible.

If you're new to the Craft, *Wicca Starter Kit* contains three of Lisa's most popular books for beginning Wiccans. You can download it for free at:

www.wiccaliving.com/free-wiccan-audiobooks

Or, if you're wanting to expand your magical skills, check out *Spellbook Starter Kit,* with three collections of spellwork featuring the powerful energies of candles, colors, crystals, mineral stones, and magical herbs. Download over 150 spells for free at:

www.wiccaliving.com/free-spell-audiobooks

Members receive free audiobooks every month, as well as exclusive discounts. And, if you don't want to continue with Audible, just remember to cancel your membership. You won't be charged a cent, and you'll get to keep your books!

Happy listening!

MORE BOOKS BY
LISA CHAMBERLAIN

Wicca for Beginners: A Guide to Wiccan Beliefs, Rituals, Magic, and Witchcraft

Wicca Book of Spells: A Book of Shadows for Wiccans, Witches, and Other Practitioners of Magic

Wicca Herbal Magic: A Beginner's Guide to Practicing Wiccan Herbal Magic, with Simple Herb Spells

Wicca Book of Herbal Spells: A Book of Shadows for Wiccans, Witches, and Other Practitioners of Herbal Magic

Wicca Candle Magic: A Beginner's Guide to Practicing Wiccan Candle Magic, with Simple Candle Spells

Wicca Book of Candle Spells: A Book of Shadows for Wiccans, Witches, and Other Practitioners of Candle Magic

Wicca Crystal Magic: A Beginner's Guide to Practicing Wiccan Crystal Magic, with Simple Crystal Spells

Wicca Book of Crystal Spells: A Book of Shadows for Wiccans, Witches, and Other Practitioners of Crystal Magic

Tarot for Beginners: A Guide to Psychic Tarot Reading, Real Tarot Card Meanings, and Simple Tarot Spreads

Runes for Beginners: A Guide to Reading Runes in Divination, Rune Magic, and the Meaning of the Elder Futhark Runes

Wicca Moon Magic: A Wiccan's Guide and Grimoire for Working Magic with Lunar Energies

Wicca Wheel of the Year Magic: A Beginner's Guide to the Sabbats, with History, Symbolism, Celebration Ideas, and Dedicated Sabbat Spells

Wicca Kitchen Witchery: A Beginner's Guide to Magical Cooking, with Simple Spells and Recipes

Wicca Essential Oils Magic: A Beginner's Guide to Working with Magical Oils, with Simple Recipes and Spells

Wicca Elemental Magic: A Guide to the Elements, Witchcraft, and Magical Spells

Wicca Magical Deities: A Guide to the Wiccan God and Goddess, and Choosing a Deity to Work Magic With

Wicca Living a Magical Life: A Guide to Initiation and Navigating Your Journey in the Craft

Magic and the Law of Attraction: A Witch's Guide to the Magic of Intention, Raising Your Frequency, and Building Your Reality

Wicca Altar and Tools: A Beginner's Guide to Wiccan Altars, Tools for Spellwork, and Casting the Circle

Wicca Finding Your Path: A Beginner's Guide to Wiccan Traditions, Solitary Practitioners, Eclectic Witches, Covens, and Circles

Wicca Book of Shadows: A Beginner's Guide to Keeping Your Own Book of Shadows and the History of Grimoires

Modern Witchcraft and Magic for Beginners: A Guide to Traditional and Contemporary Paths, with Magical Techniques for the Beginner Witch

FREE GIFT REMINDER

Just a reminder that Lisa is giving away an exclusive, free spell book as a thank-you gift to new readers!

Little Book of Spells contains ten spells that are ideal for newcomers to the practice of magic, but are also suitable for any level of experience.

Read it on read on your laptop, phone, tablet, Kindle or Nook device by visiting:

www.wiccaliving.com/bonus

DID YOU ENJOY
MODERN WITCHCRAFT
AND MAGIC FOR BEGINNERS?

Thanks so much for reading this book! I know there are many great books out there about Wicca, so I really appreciate you choosing this one.

If you enjoyed the book, I have a small favor to ask—would you take a couple of minutes to leave a review for this book on Amazon?

Your feedback will help me to make improvements to this book, and to create even better ones in the future. It will also help me develop new ideas for books on other topics that might be of interest to you. Thanks in advance for your help!

Made in the USA
Columbia, SC
15 November 2022

71295923R00088